2017 SUPPLEMENT TO MODERN CONSTITUTIONAL LAW

CASES AND NOTES

Unabridged and Abridged Eleventh Editions

■ ■ ■

Ronald D. Rotunda
Doy & Dee Henley Chair and
Distinguished Professor of Jurisprudence
Dale E. Fowler School of Law
Chapman University

AMERICAN CASEBOOK SERIES®

WEST ACADEMIC PUBLISHING

Printed in the United States of America

ISBN: 978-1-68328-964-7

To Nora and Jack

PREFACE

Since the publication of 11th editions of Modern Constitutional Law (both unabridged and abridged versions), the Court has been busy—though busier during the 2014 term than it was during the 2015 term (which ended in late June 2016). That is because the unexpected death of Justice Antonin Scalia left an even-numbered Court (eight Justices), so we had no 5 to 4 decisions. We now have a full bench and we will see more 5 to 4 decisions. President Donald J. Trump nominated Neil McGill Gorsuch on January 31, 2017. The Senate confirmed him on April 7 (54 Senators in favor; 45 opposed), and he assumed the bench on April 10, 2017.

This Supplement includes the decision of the Court, issued on its last day, allowing President Trump's Administration to bar certain aliens seeking entry into the United States, in *Trump v. International Refugee Assistance Project* (June 26, 2017). Although this case only stays the lower court injunctions, with the Court to decide the merits in the coming Term, this issue has become so newsworthy that students should read it for themselves.

The 2014 term was significant, with the Court holding (5 to 4) that there is a constitutional right to same-sex marriage, *Obergefell v. Hodges*, 576 U.S. ___, 135 S.Ct. 2584, 192 L.Ed.2d 609 (2015). The 2015 term produced several important contributions to the continued development of Constitutional Law, though no blockbusters on the order of *Obergefell*. With the 2016 term, we now have (since April 2017) a full court of nine justices.

What is significant about the 2015 term is what the Court did not decide. In *Friedrichs v. California Teachers Association*, 578 U.S. ___, 136 S.Ct. 1083, 194 L.Ed.2d 255 (2016)(per curiam), commentators widely thought that the Court would hold that the state violates free speech (1) when it requires state employees to either join the union or pay "fair share" fees to the union, and (2) when it requires state employees affirmatively to object to subsidizing non-union collective bargaining speech by public-sector unions, rather than requiring that employees affirmatively consent to subsidizing such speech. No blockbuster here. Instead, an equally divided Court affirmed the Ninth Circuit (which upheld the agency shop), creating no precedent, although handing public sector unions a major victory.

In the wake of *Obergefell* are a series of questions relating to free exercise of religion and free speech. In particular, can the federal government force non-profit religious groups to pay for health insurance that includes abortion-inducing drugs? Various religious groups, including the Little Sisters of the Poor, objected on religious and statutory grounds to facilitating abortions. In *Zubik v. Burwell*, 578 U.S. ___, 136 S.Ct. 1557, 194 L. Ed. 2d 696 (2016)(per curiam), the Court, after oral argument and supplemental briefing, vacated and remanded the case with a suggestion that the parties could settle the issue given the government concessions. While the litigation continues, the government cannot force the religious groups to fund abortifacients.

On June 26, 2017, the last day of the 2016 term, the Supreme Court agreed to consider whether the Constitution's religion clauses allow a bakery to deny service to same sex couples. Also, on the last day, the Court, in *Pavan v. Smith*, summarily reversed the Arkansas Supreme Court and decided, *per curiam*, that Arkansas' birth certificate scheme violates the Court's holding in *Obergefell v. Hodges* (2015) because it does not compel the State to issue birth certificates that name both spouses in same-sex marriages

In *United States v. Texas*, 579 U.S. ___, 136 S.Ct. 2271, 195 L.Ed.2d 638 (2016)(per curiam), the evenly divided Court affirmed the Fifth Circuit, which had affirmed the preliminary injunction of the trial court. This injunction prohibits the Obama administration (without approval from Congress) from implementing the President's executive order changing the immigration status of millions of undocumented aliens, giving them lawful presence, work permits, driver's licenses, Social Security, and other government benefits (costing an estimated $324 million over the next three years, according to the district court).

While these issues will remain for another day, they will not go away, so expect the Court to revisit them in the coming years (or, perhaps, in the coming months). Personally, I welcomed this relative quiescence of the Court when it had an even number of justices. It made the last few weeks of June a little less hectic for me. (Admittedly, this comment is a bit self-absorbed.) I still have enough to do to keep me out of mischief, not only on this book but also on the six-volume Treatise on Constitutional Law* that I coauthor with John Nowak, to whom I dedicate this book.

It is no simple task to read and edit promptly, the most recent cases of the U.S. Supreme Court and then prepare the final product for speedy publication in August, in time for the fall Constitutional Law courses. It does not help that the Court typically issues its more controversial opinions at the end of the term (late June or early July). Each term ends with a bang, not a whimper.

---

* Ronald D. Rotunda & John E. Nowak, Treatise on Constitutional Law: Substance and Procedure (5th ed., Westlaw Thomson Reuters 2012–2013)(with annual pocket parts)(6 volumes). See also, John E. Nowak & Ronald D. Rotunda, Constitutional Law (West Pub., West Hornbook Series, 8th ed. 2010), and Ronald D. Rotunda & John E. Nowak, Principles of Constitutional Law (West Academic, Concise Hornbook Series, 5th ed. 2016).

Fortunately, computers, network links, Westlaw, and high-speed modems have made my task easier. I can download an entire case within an hour after the Supreme Court releases it. The entire process is akin to magic. I used to think that computers, like telephones, were the devil's invention. Now, although they are becoming friendlier, they do not always work: like dogs, they sense fear, so I must approach them with both bravado and braggadocio. Modern technology means that old dogs like me have to learn new tricks.

I need more than computers to help me. I am grateful to John E. Nowak, the David C. Baum Professor Emeritus at the University of Illinois College of Law, for his essential advice and intellect. I also am very thankful to the many people at West Academic who make this book possible, in particular, Bonnie Karlen, Heather Sieve, and Laura Holle. And, I thank my faculty assistant, Maria Sanchez, and Drake Mirsch, J.D. 2019.

Bismarck said that laws are like sausages—one should not see how they are made. As tastes change and less filler is added to the making of sausage, some people fear that more is being added to the making of laws. Well, I have seen sausage being made (for two summers, while working the graveyard shift at a meat packing plant), and I have seen the Court make law. It is not like making sausage. Instead, our state and federal courts have protected our system of Constitutional liberties and made us the envy of the world. When we talk of imports and exports, we usually think of such things as farm goods, automobiles, and intellectual property. However, our greatest export is our Bill of Rights, which is why, when people around the world seek to preserve freedom, they often seek to emulate our judicial system.

R.D.R.

Orange, Calif.
July 2017

SUMMARY OF CONTENTS

PREFACE V

TABLE OF CASES XIII

PHOTOGRAPH OF THE SUPREME COURT XV

Chapter 1. Judicial Review 1
1–2 Limitations on the Exercise of Judicial Review 1

Chapter 4. Federal Powers Under the Commerce Clause 3
4–4 Modern Commerce Clause Cases 3

Chapter 5. The President and Congress 5
5–1 The Foundations of the Foreign Affairs Power 5
5–3 Admission and Deportation of Aliens 6

Chapter 6. Due Process 15
6–3 The New Procedural Due Process 15
6–6 The Taking of Property [Unabridged] 16
6–7 The Taking of Property [Abridged] 16
6–7 The Second Amendment [Unabridged] 17
6–8 The Second Amendment [Abridged] 17

Chapter 8. Equal Protection 19
8–2 Suspect Classes and Other Classifications 19
8–3 Fundamental Rights 20

Chapter 10. Freedom of Speech 39
10–3 Time, Place, and Manner Restrictions and the Public Forum 39
10–4 Fighting Words and Hostile Audiences 43
10–9 The Right of Association 43
10–11 Campaign Speech and Financing 44

Chapter 11. Religion 47
11–3 Religiously Based Exceptions to State Imposed Duties 47

Chapter 12. The Procedural Context of Constitutional Litigation 61
12–4 Nontaxpayer Standing 61

TABLE OF CONTENTS

PREFACE V

TABLE OF CASES XIII

PHOTOGRAPH OF THE SUPREME COURT XV

Chapter 1. Judicial Review 1
1–2 Limitations on the Exercise of Judicial Review 1
1–2.2 Statutory Restrictions 1

Chapter 4. Federal Powers Under the Commerce Clause 3
4–4 Modern Commerce Clause Cases 3

Chapter 5. The President and Congress 5
5–1 The Foundations of the Foreign Affairs Power 5
5–1.1 Historical Foundations 5
5–3 Admission and Deportation of Aliens 6
Trump v. International Refugee Assistance Project 7

Chapter 6. Due Process 15
6–3 The New Procedural Due Process 15
6–3.2 Determining What Process Is Due 15
6–6 The Taking of Property [Unabridged] 16
6–7 The Taking of Property [Abridged] 16
6–6.1 Taking by Possession [Unabridged] 16
6–7.1 Taking by Possession [Abridged] 16
6–7 The Second Amendment [Unabridged] 17
6–8 The Second Amendment [Abridged] 17

Chapter 8. Equal Protection 19
8–2 Suspect Classes and Other Classifications 19
8–2.1 Race 19
8–2.14 Reverse Discrimination 19
8–2.14.1 Education 19
8–3 Fundamental Rights 20
8–3.2 Voting [Unabridged] 20
8–3.1 Voting [Abridged] 20
8–3.21 Apportionment [Unabridged] 20
8–3.11 Apportionment [Abridged] 20
8–3.4 Privacy and Sexual Autonomy [Unabridged] 21
8–3.3 Privacy and Sexual Autonomy [Abridged] 21
8–3.43 Abortion [Unabridged] 21
8–3.33 Abortion [Abridged] 21
8–3.44 Homosexuality [Unabridged] 24

8–3.34 Homosexuality [Abridged] 24
Obergefell v. Hodges 24
Notes 35

Chapter 10. Freedom of Speech 39
10–3 Time, Place, and Manner Restrictions and the Public Forum 39
10–3.3 Defining the Public Forum [Unabridged] 39
10–3.2 Defining the Public Forum [Abridged] 39
10–3.4 Government Subsidization of Speech [Unabridged] 41
10–3.3 Government Subsidization of Speech [Abridged] 41
10–4 Fighting Words and Hostile Audiences 43
10–9 The Right of Association 43
10–9.3 Patronage Dismissals 43
10–11 Campaign Speech and Financing 44

Chapter 11. Religion 47
11–3 Religiously Based Exceptions to State Imposed Duties 47
Trinity Lutheran Church of Columbia, Inc. v. Comer 49
Notes 58

Chapter 12. The Procedural Context of Constitutional Litigation 61
12–4 Nontaxpayer Standing 61
12–4.3 Congressional Standing 61

TABLE OF CASES

The principal cases are in bold type.

Arizona State Legislature v. Arizona Independent Redistricting Commission, 61
Baker v. Nelson, 26
Bank Markazi v. Peterson, 1
Bowers v. Hardwick, 26
Brown v. Buhman, 31, 36
Caetano v. Massachusetts, 17
Church of Lukumi Babalu Aye, Inc. v. Hialeah, 51
Colorado State Board of Education v. Taxpayers for Public Education, 59
Elonis v. United States, 43
Evenwel v. Abbott, 20
Everson v. Board of Education of Ewing, 51
Fiallo v. Bell, 6
Fisher v. University of Texas, 19
Friedrichs v. California Teachers Association, v
Heart of Atlanta Motel, Inc. v. United States, 35
Heffernan v. City of Patterson, 43
Holder v. Humanitarian Law Project, 12
Holt v. Hobbs, 47
Horne v. Department of Agriculture, 16
Hurley v. Irish-American Gay, Lesbian and Bisexual Group of Boston, 36
King v. Burwell, 3
Kleindienst v. Mandel, 10, 11
Lawrence v. Texas, 26
Lee v. Tam, 42
Lochner v. New York, 31
Locke v. Davey, 51, 56, 57
Loving v. Virginia, 26
Lyng v. Northwest Indian Cemetery Protective Association, 52
Matal v. Tam, 42
McDaniel v. Paty, 51
Nelson v. Colorado, 15
New Mexico Ass'n of Non-public Schools v. Moses, 59
Obergefell v. Hodges, v, **24**
Packingham v. North Carolina, 40
Pavan v. Smith, 37
Reed v. Town of Gilbert, 39
Roe v. Wade, 36
Romer v. Evans, 26
Runyon v. McCrary, 35
Sessions v. Morales-Santana, 6
Skinner v. Oklahoma ex rel. Williamson, 26
Texas, United States v., vi
Trinity Lutheran Church of Columbia, Inc. v. Comer, 49
Trump v. International Refugee Assistance Project, 7
Turner v. Safley, 26
Voisine v. United States, 17
Walker v. Texas Division, Sons of Confederate Veterans, Inc., 41
Washington v. Trump, 7, 8
Whole Woman's Health v. Hellerstedt, 21
Williams-Yulee v. Florida Bar, 44
Wisconsin v. Yoder, 51
Wooley v. Maynard, 41
Zablocki v. Redhail, 26
Zivotofsky v. Kerry, 5
Zubik v. Burwell, vi, 47, 48

June 1, 2017. Seated, from the left: Associate Justice Ruth Bader Ginsburg, Associate Justice Anthony Kennedy, Chief Justice John Roberts, Associate Justice Clarence Thomas, and Associate Justice Stephen Breyer. Standing, from left: Associate Justice Elena Kagan, Associate Justice Samuel Alito Jr., Associate Justice Sonia Sotomayor, and Associate Justice Neil Gorsuch.

2017 SUPPLEMENT TO

MODERN CONSTITUTIONAL LAW

CASES AND NOTES

Unabridged and Abridged
Eleventh Editions

CHAPTER 1

JUDICIAL REVIEW

■ ■ ■

1–2 LIMITATIONS ON THE EXERCISE OF JUDICIAL REVIEW

1–2.2 STATUTORY RESTRICTIONS

Unabridged, p. 41; add to end of *Notes*, new Note 5:

Abridged, p. 40; add to end of *Notes*, new Note 5:

5. *Bank Markazi v. Peterson,* 578 U.S. ____, 136 S.Ct. 1310, 194 L.Ed.2d 464 (2016). Bank Markazi is the Central Bank of Iran. Respondents included more than 1,000 victims of Iran-sponsored acts of terrorism, their estate representatives, and surviving family members. They sued Iran for terrorist acts. To enforce judgments they obtained by default, they moved for turnover of about $1.75 billion in bond assets held in a New York bank account. Respondents alleged that Bank Markazi, the Central Bank of Iran owned these assets.

When Respondents learned of bonds in a New York bank that the U.S. Government had frozen, they went after them. The turnover began in 2008. In 2012, Congress enacted the Iran Threat Reduction and Syria Human Rights Act of 2012. 22 U.S.C. § 8772. That statute makes a designated set of assets available to satisfy the judgments underlying a consolidated enforcement proceeding, which the statute specifically identifies by the District Court's docket number. Section 8772(a)(2) requires a court to determine, before allowing execution against these assets, "whether Iran holds equitable title to, or the beneficial interest in, the assets." Justice Ginsburg, for the Court, held that § 8772, is constitutional.

Bank Markazi argued that § 8772 violate separation of powers by purporting to change the law and direct a particular result in, a single pending case. Ginsburg admitted that § 8772 "is an unusual statute: It designates a particular set of assets and renders them available to satisfy the liability and damages judgments underlying a consolidated enforcement proceeding that the statute identifies by the District Court's docket number." However, this law simply facilitates execution of judgments in 16 suits. While Congress may not force the courts to reopen final judgments, it has the power to make valid statutes retroactively applicable to pending cases. Moreover, § 8772 is an exercise of congressional authority regarding foreign affairs, where the controlling role of the political bodies is both necessary and proper.

Roberts, C.J., dissenting (joined by Sotomayor, J.) acknowledged, "the rule that courts generally must apply a retroactively applicable statute to pending cases." Still, he argued, this law violates separation of powers because "Congress has decided this case by enacting a bespoke statute tailored to this case that resolves the parties' specific legal disputes to guarantee respondents victory."

CHAPTER 4

FEDERAL POWERS UNDER THE COMMERCE CLAUSE

■ ■ ■

4–4 MODERN COMMERCE CLAUSE CASES

Unabridged, p. 302; add to end of *Notes*, new Note 8:

Abridged, p. 264; add to end of *Notes*, new Note 8:

8. *King v. Burwell*, 576 U.S. ___, 135 S.Ct. 2480, 192 L.Ed.2d 483 (2015). This case is significant although it relates to statutory interpretation, not the Commerce Clause. The Affordable Care Act (ACA) provides that if a state set up a "qualified health exchange," then the insureds qualify for generous federal subsidies. If a state refuses to do that, the law authorizes the Secretary of Health and Human Services (HHS) to set up Federal Exchanges. No provision of the ACA offers any tax subsidies for *federally* created (as opposed to *state* created) Health Exchanges. If the state refuses to create a Health Exchange that state's citizens do not receive these financial subsidies, but they still have to pay federal taxes that finance the subsidies that residents in other states (those with state-created Exchanges) will receive.

No section of the ACA defines "State" to include the federal government; other sections define "State" to include the 50 states, the District of Columbia, and U.S. territories, e.g., Guam. To the surprise of many ACA supporters, only 16 States and the District of Columbia established their own Exchanges. Given that so many states did not enact qualified exchanges, the IRS issued a regulation interpreting the relevant language to provide that "regardless of whether the Exchange is established and operated by a State . . . or by HHS," the subsidies are available. Roberts, C.J. for the Court (6 to 3), held that that Congress did not intend to delegate to the IRS the power to issue such an interpretation but the statutory language was ambiguous, and so the Court will interpret it. The Court conceded that "The Affordable Care Act contains more than a few examples of inartful drafting," and "arguments about the plain meaning of Section 36B are strong." Nonetheless, in light of the "broader structure of the Act," these subsidies are necessary and that "compels us to reject petitioners' interpretation because it would destabilize the individual insurance market in any State with a Federal Exchange, and likely create the very 'death spirals' that Congress designed the Act to avoid." Because the Court did not accept the Solicitor General's argument to defer to the IRS, a future IRS under a different Administration cannot change the interpretation of this law.

Scalia, J., joined by Thomas & Alito, JJ., dissented. "The Court holds that when the [ACA] says 'Exchange established by the State' it means 'Exchange established by the State or the Federal Government.' That is of course quite absurd, and the Court's 21 pages of explanation make it no less so." Words have no meaning if an Exchange "*not* established by a State is 'established by the State.' " "We lack the prerogative to repair laws that do not work out in practice, just as the people lack the ability to throw us out of office if they dislike the solutions we concoct." The Court attempts "to palm off the pertinent statutory phrase as 'inartful drafting' " but it "does not pretend" that there is any "drafting error on the face of § 36B." For this Court, "normal rules of interpretation seem always to yield to the overriding principle of the present Court: The Affordable Care Act must be saved." The Court has engaged in "interpretive jiggery-pokery," and thus, "We should start calling this law SCOTUScare." (SCOTUS stands for Supreme Court of the United States.)*

* For further discussion (pardon the shameless self-promotion), see, Rotunda, *King v. Burwell and the Rise of the Administrative State*, 23 U. MIAMI BUSINESS REV. 267 (2015).

CHAPTER 5

THE PRESIDENT AND CONGRESS

■ ■ ■

5–1 THE FOUNDATIONS OF THE FOREIGN AFFAIRS POWER

5–1.1 HISTORICAL FOUNDATIONS

Unabridged, p. 353; add to end of *Notes*, new Note 6:

Abridged, p. 302; add to end of *Notes*, new Note 6:

6. *Zivotofsky v. Kerry*, 576 U.S. ___, 135 S.Ct. 2076, 192 L. Ed. 2d 83 (2015). Zivotofsky was born to United States citizens living in Jerusalem. His parents, on his behalf, sued the Secretary of State for declaratory and injunctive relief, arguing that the child was entitled—pursuant to the Foreign Relations Authorization Act (FRAA)—to have "Israel" listed as his place of birth on his U.S. passport. Instead, pursuant to State Department policy, the passport would list only "Jerusalem." Justice Kennedy, for the Court, held (6 to 3) that this law violated the President's exclusive power to recognize foreign nations and governments, Art. II, § 3. The Executive Branch's longstanding position is that the United States "does not recognize any country as having sovereignty over Jerusalem."

Thomas, J. (concurring in the judgment and dissenting in part) concluded that § 214(d) was unconstitutional "insofar as it directs the President, contrary to his wishes, to list 'Israel' as the place of birth of Jerusalem-born citizens on their passports." That is because the "President has long regulated passports under his residual foreign affairs power." However, "§ 214(d) poses no such problem insofar as it regulates consular reports of birth abroad." "The regulation of these reports does not fall within the President's foreign affairs powers, but within Congress' enumerated powers under the Naturalization and Necessary and Proper Clauses."

Roberts, C.J., joined by Alito, J., dissented. "Never before has this Court accepted a President's direct defiance of an Act of Congress in the field of foreign affairs. We have instead stressed that the President's power reaches 'its lowest ebb, when he contravenes the express will of Congress, 'for what is at stake is the equilibrium established by our constitutional system,' " quoting Justice Jackson's concurrence in *Youngstown*. Scalia, J., joined by Roberts, C.J., & Alito, J., also dissented, noting that eleven of the powers that Article I, § 8 grants Congress deal in some way with foreign affairs. Section 214(d) "has nothing to do with recognition" of a foreign sovereign. It does not require the

"Secretary to make a formal declaration about Israel's sovereignty over Jerusalem." Birthplace designation on a passport has nothing to do with exchanges of ambassadors.

5–3 ADMISSION AND DEPORTATION OF ALIENS

Unabridged (only), p. 406; add to *Notes*, new Note 4:

4. *Sessions v. Morales-Santana,* 582 U.S. ___, 137 S.Ct. 1678, ___ L.Ed.2d ___, 2017 WL 2507339 (2017). Son born abroad to an unwed citizen father and a non-citizen mother sought to reopen his removal proceedings to evaluate his claim of derivative citizenship. The Immigration and Nationality Act allows for acquisition of U.S. citizenship from birth by a child born abroad, when one parent is a U.S. citizen and the other is not, under certain circumstances. If the U.S.-citizen parent must have ten years' physical presence in the United States prior to the child's birth, "at least five of which were after attaining" age 14. However, if the child seeks citizenship through his unwed U.S.-citizen mother, the mother can transmit her citizenship to her child born abroad if she has lived continuously in the United States for just one year prior to the child's birth. The Government sought to remove Morales-Santana based on several criminal convictions, and treated him as alien because he sought citizenship through his citizen-father. He would have qualified if the law treated his citizen-father the same as the citizen-mother.

Ginsburg, J., for the Court, held that the gender line that Congress drew violates the Fifth Amendment's requirement that the Government accord to all persons "the equal protection of the laws." The Court distinguished *Fiallo v. Bell*, 430 U.S. 787, 97 S.Ct. 1473, 52 L.Ed.2d 50 (1977) because *Fiallo* involved entry preferences for alien children; the case did not present a claim of U.S. citizenship. This sex-based distinction between unwed fathers and unwed mothers (premised on the archaic view that unwed fathers care less about their children than unwed mothers do) is unconstitutional.

However, the Court stated that it is not equipped to convert the one-year exception for unwed mothers into the main rule. Congress must decide that issue. Ordinarily "the preferred rule" is to extend favorable treatment to the excluded class rather than withdrawing favorable treatment from the favored class. However, extending the one-year rule for unwed mothers to unwed fathers would displace Congress' general rule that requires longer physical presence. Therefore, the Court held it would adopt the rule that Congress would likely have chosen—to apply the longer five-year requirement of the general rule prospectively to children born to unwed citizen mothers. "Going forward, Congress may address the issue and settle on a uniform prescription that neither favors nor disadvantages any person on the basis of gender. In the interim, as the Government suggests, § 1401(a)(7)'s now-five-year requirement should apply, prospectively, to children born to unwed U.S.-citizen mothers."

Thomas, J., joined by Alito, J., concurred in the judgment, and said, "I am skeptical that we even have the 'power to provide relief of the sort requested in this suit—namely, conferral of citizenship on a basis other than that prescribed by Congress.' "

Unabridged, p. 406; at end of *Notes*, add new case:

Abridged, p. 330; at end of *Notes*, add new case:

TRUMP V. INTERNATIONAL REFUGEE ASSISTANCE PROJECT

582 U.S. ___, 137 S.Ct. 2080, ___ L.Ed.2d ___, 2017 WL 2722580 (2017).

On Application for Stay and Petition for Writ of Certiorari to The United States Court of Appeals for The Fourth Circuit

PER CURIAM.

These cases involve challenges to Executive Order No. 13780, Protecting the Nation From Foreign Terrorist Entry Into the United States. The order alters practices concerning the entry of foreign nationals into the United States by, among other things, suspending entry of nationals from six designated countries for 90 days. Respondents challenged the order in two separate lawsuits. They obtained preliminary injunctions barring enforcement of several of its provisions, including the 90-day suspension of entry. The injunctions were upheld in large measure by the Courts of Appeals.

The Government filed separate petitions for certiorari, as well as applications to stay the preliminary injunctions entered by the lower courts. We grant the petitions for certiorari and grant the stay applications in part.

On January 27, 2017, President Donald J. Trump signed Executive Order No. 13769, Protecting the Nation From Foreign Terrorist Entry Into the United States. 82 Fed.Reg. 8977 (EO–1). EO–1 addressed policies and procedures relating to the entry of foreign nationals into this country. Among other directives, the order suspended entry of foreign nationals from seven countries identified as presenting heightened terrorism risks—Iran, Iraq, Libya, Somalia, Sudan, Syria, and Yemen—for 90 days. § 3(c). Executive officials were instructed to review the adequacy of current practices relating to visa adjudications during this 90-day period. § 3(a). EO–1 also modified refugee policy, suspending the United States Refugee Admissions Program (USRAP) for 120 days and reducing the number of refugees eligible to be admitted to the United States during fiscal year 2017.

EO–1 was immediately challenged in court. Just a week after the order was issued, a Federal District Court entered a nationwide temporary restraining order enjoining enforcement of several of its key provisions. *Washington v. Trump,* 2017 WL 462040 (W.D.Wash., Feb.3, 2017). Six days later, the Court of Appeals for the Ninth Circuit denied the Government's emergency motion to stay the order pending appeal. *Washington v. Trump*, 847 F.3d 1151 (2017). Rather than continue to litigate EO–1, the Government announced that it would revoke the order and issue a new one.

A second order followed on March 6, 2017. See Protecting the Nation From Foreign Terrorist Entry Into the United States, Exec. Order No. 13780, 82 Fed.Reg. 13209 (EO–2). EO–2 describes "conditions in six of the . . . countries" as to which EO–1 had suspended entry, stating that these conditions "demonstrate [that] nationals [of those countries] continue to present heightened risks to the security of the United States," § 1(e), and that "some of those who have entered the United States through our immigration system have proved to be threats to our national security," § 1(h).

Having identified these concerns, EO–2 sets out a series of directives patterned on those found in EO–1. Several are relevant here. First, EO–2 directs the Secretary of Homeland Security to conduct a global review to determine whether foreign governments provide adequate information about nationals applying for United States visas. § 2(a). EO–2 directs the Secretary to report his findings to the President within 20 days of the order's "effective date," after which time those nations identified as deficient will be given 50 days to alter their practices.

Second, EO–2 directs that entry of nationals from six of the seven countries designated in EO–1—Iran, Libya, Somalia, Sudan, Syria, and Yemen—be "suspended for 90 days from the effective date" of the order. § 2(c). EO–2 explains that this pause is necessary to ensure that dangerous individuals do not enter the United States while the Executive is working to establish "adequate standards . . . to prevent infiltration by foreign terrorists"; in addition, suspending entry will "temporarily reduce investigative burdens on agencies" during the Secretary's 20-day review. *Ibid.* A separate section provides for case-by-case waivers of the entry bar. § 3(c).

Third, EO–2 suspends "decisions on applications for refugee status" and "travel of refugees into the United States under the USRAP" for 120 days following its effective date. § 6(a). During that period, the Secretary of State is instructed to review the adequacy of USRAP application and adjudication procedures and implement whatever additional procedures are necessary "to ensure that individuals seeking admission as refugees do not pose a threat" to national security.

Fourth, citing the President's determination that "the entry of more than 50,000 refugees in fiscal year 2017 would be detrimental to the interests of the United States," EO–2 "suspend[s] any entries in excess of that number" for this fiscal year. § 6(b).

Finally, § 14 of EO–2 establishes the order's effective date: March 16, 2017.

Respondents in these cases filed separate lawsuits challenging EO–2. As relevant, they argued that the order violates the Establishment Clause of the First Amendment because it was motivated not by concerns pertaining to national security, but by animus toward Islam. They further argued that EO–2 does not comply with certain provisions in the Immigration and Nationality Act (INA), 66 Stat. 187, as amended. . . .

The Court of Appeals for the Fourth Circuit ruled first. On May 25, over three dissenting votes, the en banc court issued a decision in *IRAP* that largely upheld the order enjoining enforcement of § 2(c). The majority determined that respondent John Doe # 1, a lawful permanent resident whose Iranian wife is seeking entry to the United States, was likely to succeed on the merits of his Establishment Clause claim. The majority concluded that the primary purpose of § 2(c) was religious, in violation of the First Amendment: A reasonable observer familiar with all the circumstances—including the predominantly Muslim character of the designated countries and statements made by President Trump during his Presidential campaign—would conclude that § 2(c) was motivated principally by a desire to exclude Muslims from the United States, not by considerations relating to national security. Having reached this conclusion, the court upheld the preliminary injunction prohibiting enforcement of § 2(c) against any foreign national seeking to enter this country. . . .

Respondents' June 12 filings injected a new issue into the cases. In *IRAP,* respondents argued that the suspension of entry in § 2(c) would expire on June 14. [They argued that], even though it had never been enforced, the entry suspension would expire 90 days from March 16: June 14. At that time, the dispute over § 2(c) would become moot. Brief in Opposition 13–14.

On the same day respondents filed, the Ninth Circuit ruled in *Hawaii.* ___ F.3d ___, 2017 WL 2529640 (June 12, 2017) (*per curiam*). A unanimous panel held in favor of respondents the State of Hawaii and Dr. Ismail Elshikh, an American citizen and imam whose Syrian mother-in-law is seeking entry to this country. Rather than rely on the constitutional grounds supporting the District Court's decision, the court held that portions of EO–2 likely exceeded the President's authority under the INA. On that basis it upheld the injunction as to the § 2(c) entry suspension, the § 6(a) suspension of refugee admissions, and the § 6(b) refugee cap. The Ninth Circuit, like the Fourth Circuit, concluded that the injunction should bar enforcement of these provisions across the board, because they would violate the INA "in all applications." *Id.*, at *28. The court did, however, narrow the injunction so that it would not bar the Government from undertaking the internal executive reviews directed by EO–2.

We granted the parties' requests for supplemental briefing addressed to the decision of the Ninth Circuit. Before those briefs were filed, however, the ground shifted again. On June 14, evidently in response to the argument that § 2(c) was about to expire, President Trump issued a memorandum to Executive Branch officials. The memorandum declared the effective date of each enjoined provision of EO–2 to be the date on which the injunctions in these cases "are lifted or stayed with respect to that provision." The memorandum further provided that, to the extent necessary, it "should be construed to amend the Executive Order." *Ibid.* The Government takes the view that, if any mootness problem existed previously, the President's memorandum has cured it. . . .

The Government seeks review on several issues. In *IRAP,* the Government argues that respondent Doe lacks standing to challenge § 2(c).[*] The Government also contends that Doe's Establishment Clause claim fails on the merits. In its view, the Fourth Circuit should not have asked whether § 2(c) has a primarily religious purpose. The court instead should have upheld EO–2 because it rests on the "facially legitimate and bona fide" justification of protecting national security. *Kleindienst v. Mandel,* 408 U.S. 753, 770, 92 S.Ct. 2576, 33 L.Ed.2d 683 (1972). In addition, the Fourth Circuit erred by focusing on the President's campaign-trail comments to conclude that § 2(c)—religiously neutral on its face—nonetheless has a principally religious purpose. At the very least, the Government argues, the injunction is too broad.

In *Hawaii,* the Government likewise argues that respondents Hawaii and Dr. Elshikh lack standing and that (at a minimum) the injunction should be narrowed. The Government's principal merits contention pertains to a statutory provision authorizing the President to "suspend the entry of all aliens or any class of aliens" to this country "[w]henever [he] finds that the entry of any aliens or of any class of aliens . . . would be detrimental to the interests of the United States." 8 U.S.C. § 1182(f). The Ninth Circuit held that "[t]here is no sufficient finding in [EO–2] that the entry of the excluded classes would be detrimental to the interests of the United States." *Hawaii,* 2017 WL 2529640, at *14. This, the Government argues, constitutes impermissible judicial second-guessing of the President's judgment on a matter of national security.

In addition to seeking certiorari, the Government asks the Court to stay the injunctions entered below, thereby permitting the enjoined provisions to take effect. According to the Government, it is likely to suffer irreparable harm unless a stay issues. Focusing mostly on § 2(c), and pointing to the descriptions of conditions in the six designated nations, the Government argues that a 90-day pause on entry is necessary to prevent potentially dangerous individuals from entering the United States while the Executive reviews the adequacy of information provided by foreign governments in connection with visa adjudications. Additionally, the Government asserts, the temporary bar is needed to reduce the Executive's investigative burdens while this review proceeds.

To begin, we grant both of the Government's petitions for certiorari and consolidate the cases for argument. The Clerk is directed to set a briefing schedule that will permit the cases to be heard during the first session of October Term 2017. (The Government has not requested that we expedite consideration of the merits to a greater extent.) In addition to the issues identified in the petitions, the parties are directed to address the following question: "Whether the challenges to § 2(c) became moot on June 14, 2017."

We now turn to the preliminary injunctions barring enforcement of the § 2(c) entry suspension. We grant the Government's applications to stay the injunctions, to the extent the injunctions prevent enforcement of § 2(c) with respect to foreign nationals who lack any bona fide relationship with a person or entity in the United States. We leave the injunctions entered by the lower courts in place with respect to respondents and those similarly situated, as specified in this opinion. . . .

The [lower] courts approved injunctions that covered not just respondents, but parties similarly situated to them—that is, people or entities in the United States who have relationships with foreign nationals abroad, and whose rights might be affected if those foreign nationals were excluded. See *Mandel,* 408 U.S., at 763–765 (permitting American plaintiffs to challenge the exclusion of a foreign national on the ground that the exclusion violated their own First Amendment rights).

But the injunctions reach much further than that: They also bar enforcement of § 2(c) against foreign nationals abroad who have no connection to the United States at all. The equities relied on by the lower courts do not balance the same way in that context. Denying entry to such a foreign national does not burden any American party by reason of that party's relationship with the foreign national. And the courts below did not conclude that exclusion in such circumstances would impose any legally relevant hardship on the foreign national himself. See *Mandel*, at 762 ("[A]n unadmitted and nonresident alien . . . ha[s] no constitutional right of entry to this country"). So whatever burdens may result from enforcement of § 2(c) against a foreign national who lacks any connection to this country, they are, at a minimum, a good deal less concrete than the hardships identified by the courts below.

At the same time, the Government's interest in enforcing § 2(c), and the Executive's authority to do so, are undoubtedly at their peak when there is no tie between the foreign national and the United States. Indeed,

EO–2 itself distinguishes between foreign nationals who have some connection to this country, and foreign nationals who do not, by establishing a case-by-case waiver system primarily for the benefit of individuals in the former category. See, *e.g.,* §§ 3(c)(i)–(vi). The interest in preserving national security is "an urgent objective of the highest order." *Holder v. Humanitarian Law Project,* 561 U.S. 1, 28, 130 S.Ct. 2705, 177 L.Ed.2d 355 (2010). To prevent the Government from pursuing that objective by enforcing § 2(c) against foreign nationals unconnected to the United States would appreciably injure its interests, without alleviating obvious hardship to anyone else.

We accordingly grant the Government's stay applications in part and narrow the scope of the injunctions as to § 2(c). The injunctions remain in place only with respect to parties similarly situated to Doe, Dr. Elshikh, and Hawaii. In practical terms, this means that § 2(c) may not be enforced against foreign nationals who have a credible claim of a bona fide relationship with a person or entity in the United States. All other foreign nationals are subject to the provisions of EO–2.

The facts of these cases illustrate the sort of relationship that qualifies. For individuals, a close familial relationship is required. A foreign national who wishes to enter the United States to live with or visit a family member, like Doe's wife or Dr. Elshikh's mother-in-law, clearly has such a relationship. As for entities, the relationship must be formal, documented, and formed in the ordinary course, rather than for the purpose of evading EO–2. The students from the designated countries who have been admitted to the University of Hawaii have such a relationship with an American entity. So too would a worker who accepted an offer of employment from an American company or a lecturer invited to address an American audience. Not so someone who enters into a relationship simply to avoid § 2(c): For example, a nonprofit group devoted to immigration issues may not contact foreign nationals from the designated countries, add them to client lists, and then secure their entry by claiming injury from their exclusion. . . .

The *Hawaii* injunction extends beyond § 2(c) to bar enforcement of the § 6(a) suspension of refugee admissions and the § 6(b) refugee cap. In our view, the equitable balance struck above applies in this context as well. An American individual or entity that has a bona fide relationship with a particular person seeking to enter the country as a refugee can legitimately claim concrete hardship if that person is excluded. As to these individuals and entities, we do not disturb the injunction. But when it comes to refugees who lack any such connection to the United States, for the reasons we have set out, the balance tips in favor of the Government's compelling need to provide for the Nation's security.

The Government's application to stay the injunction with respect to §§ 6(a) and (b) is accordingly granted in part. Section 6(a) may not be enforced against an individual seeking admission as a refugee who can credibly claim a bona fide relationship with a person or entity in the United States. Nor may § 6(b); that is, such a person may not be excluded pursuant to § 6(b), even if the 50,000-person cap has been reached or exceeded. As applied to all other individuals, the provisions may take effect.

Accordingly, the petitions for certiorari are granted, and the stay applications are granted in part. It is so ordered.

JUSTICE THOMAS, with whom JUSTICE ALITO and JUSTICE GORSUCH join, concurring in part and dissenting in part.

I agree with the Court that the preliminary injunctions entered in these cases should be stayed, although I would stay them in full. . . . Reasonable minds may disagree on where the balance of equities lies as between the Government and respondents in these cases. It would have been reasonable, perhaps, for the Court to have left the injunctions in place only as to respondents themselves. But the Court takes the additional step of keeping the injunctions in place with regard to an unidentified, unnamed group of foreign nationals abroad. No class has been certified, and neither party asks for the scope of relief that the Court today provides. . . .

Moreover, I fear that the Court's remedy will prove unworkable. Today's compromise will burden executive officials with the task of deciding—on peril of contempt—whether individuals from the six affected nations who wish to enter the United States have a sufficient connection to a person or entity in this country. See *ante,* at 11–12. The compromise also will invite a flood of litigation until this case is finally resolved on the merits, as parties and courts struggle to determine what exactly constitutes a "bona fide relationship," who precisely has a "credible claim" to that relationship, and whether the claimed relationship was formed "simply to avoid § 2(c)" of Executive Order No. 13780, *ante,* at 11, 12. And litigation of the factual and legal issues that are likely to arise will presumably be directed to the two District Courts whose initial orders in these cases this Court has now—unanimously—found sufficiently questionable to be stayed as to the vast majority of the people potentially affected.

CHAPTER 6

DUE PROCESS

■ ■ ■

6–3 THE NEW PROCEDURAL DUE PROCESS

6–3.2 DETERMINING WHAT PROCESS IS DUE

Unabridged, p. 577; add to end of *Notes*, Note 6:

Abridged, p. 454; add to end of *Notes*, Note 3:

Nelson v. Colorado, 581 U.S. ___, 137 S.Ct. 1249, 197 L. Ed. 2d 611 (2017). In two separate cases, Colorado convicted Nelson and Madden of different crimes. The lower courts sentenced them to prison terms and payment of fees, court costs, and restitution. The state courts later reversed their convictions on appeal. At retrial, Nelson was acquitted, and the state decided not to retry Madden. Each then sought the return of fees, court costs and restitution that they had paid to the state. The Colorado Supreme Court rejected their claims because the relevant state statute requires a claimant to prove by clear and convincing evidence that he or she innocent. The Supreme Court reversed (7 to 1), applying *Mathews v. Eldridge* (1976). The relevant factors are (1) the private interest affected, (2) the risk of an erroneous deprivation of that interest, and (3) the relevant governmental interests. All three factors weighed decisively against the Colorado procedure, which therefore was unconstitutional. "Colorado may not retain funds taken from Nelson and Madden solely because of their now-invalidated convictions, for Colorado may not presume a person, adjudged guilty of no crime, nonetheless guilty enough for monetary exactions."

6–6 THE TAKING OF PROPERTY [UNABRIDGED]

6–7 THE TAKING OF PROPERTY [ABRIDGED]

6–6.1 TAKING BY POSSESSION [UNABRIDGED]

6–7.1 TAKING BY POSSESSION [ABRIDGED]

Unabridged, p. 603; add to end of *Notes*, new Note 5:

Abridged, p. 472; add to end of *Notes*, new Note 3:

Horne v. Department of Agriculture, 576 U.S. ___, 135 S.Ct. 2419, 192 L.Ed.2d 388 (2015). The Agricultural Marketing Agreement Act of 1937 authorizes the Secretary of Agriculture to promulgate "marketing orders" to help maintain stable markets for particular agricultural products. The marketing order for raisins imposed a requirement that growers set aside a certain percentage of their crop for the Government, free of charge. The Government then may sell those raisins in noncompetitive markets, donate them, or dispose of them by other means. If the Government realizes any profits (after subtracting expenses from administering the program), it distributes the net proceeds to the raisin growers. In 2002–03, it required raisin growers to set aside 47% of their raisin crop under the reserve requirement. In 2003–04, it required 30%. Horne refused to set aside any raisins arguing that the reserve requirement was an unconstitutional taking of property without just compensation. The Government fined the Hornes the fair market value of the raisins as well as additional civil penalties for their failure to obey the raisin marketing order.

The Ninth Circuit held that the reserve requirement did not violate the Fifth Amendment because personal property has less protection than real property and because the Hornes retained an interest in any net proceeds of the property. The Ninth Circuit also held that Horne could avoid relinquishing large percentages of their crop by "planting different crops." Roberts, C.J., for the Court (8 to 1) rejected both arguments and held that the Fifth Amendment applies to personal property as well as real property.

There is a classic "taking" when the Government "directly appropriates private property for its own use," whether it is real or personal property. "The Government has a categorical duty to pay just compensation when it takes your car, just as when it takes your home." The fact that Horne had a contingent interest in a portion of the raisins' value did not negate the Government's duty to pay just compensation for what it took.

The Court also rejected the Government argument that the reserve requirement is not a taking because raisin growers "voluntarily choose" to participate in the raisin market. The Government cannot take a landlord's property just because the landlord could choose a different occupation. " 'Let them sell wine' is probably not much more comforting to the raisin growers than similar retorts have been to others throughout history." Selling in interstate commerce is "not a special governmental benefit that the Government may hold hostage, to be ransomed by the waiver of constitutional protection." The Government owes "just compensation" to Horne, measured that by the market value of the property at the time of the taking. The Government fined the Hornes the fair market value of the raisins, and "it cannot now disavow that valuation." The Government must also not collect the associated civil penalty.

6–7 THE SECOND AMENDMENT [UNABRIDGED]

6–8 THE SECOND AMENDMENT [ABRIDGED]

Unabridged, p. 637; add to end of *Notes*, new Note 4:

Abridged, p. 499; add to end of *Notes*, new Note 3:

Caetano v. Massachusetts, 577 U.S. ___, 136 S.Ct. 1027, 194 L.Ed.2d 99 (2016)(per curiam). The Massachusetts Supreme Judicial Court upheld a state law prohibiting the possession of stun guns after considering "whether a stun gun is the type of weapon contemplated by Congress in 1789 as being protected by the Second Amendment." The unanimous Court reversed and held that the state court's opinion directly contradicted *District of Columbia v. Heller* (2008). "[T]he Second Amendment extends, prima facie, to all instruments that constitute bearable arms, even those that were not in existence at the time of the founding."

Alito, J., joined by Thomas, J., concurred in the judgment: The "pertinent Second Amendment inquiry is whether stun guns are commonly possessed by law-abiding citizens for lawful purposes *today*." Only seven states ban stun guns. Caetano's abusive ex-boyfriend earlier put her in the hospital and ignored multiple restraining orders. A friend gave her a stun gun. When the ex-boyfriend threatened her after she left work, she displayed the stun gun and threatened to use it unless he left. "Massachusetts was either unable or unwilling to do what was necessary to protect her." Instead, "the Commonwealth chose to deploy its prosecutorial resources to prosecute and convict her of a criminal offense for arming herself with a nonlethal weapon that may well have saved her life."

Later that same term, the Court decided, *Voisine v. United States*, 579 U.S. ___, 136 S.Ct. 2272, 195 L. Ed. 2d 736 (2016)(6 to 2). Federal law prohibits any person convicted of a "misdemeanor crime of domestic violence" from possessing a firearm. 18 U.S.C. § 922(g)(9). The statute defines that to include any misdemeanor committed against a domestic relation that necessarily involves the "use . . . of physical force." The Court held (6 to 2) that a misdemeanor assault conviction for reckless (as contrasted to knowing or intentional) conduct triggers the statutory firearms ban. Kagan, J., spoke for the Court. Recklessness "is the result of a deliberate decision to endanger another." The relevant term, "use," is "indifferent as to whether the actor has the mental state of intention, knowledge, or recklessness with respect to the harmful consequences of his volitional conduct." Congress enacted § 922(g)(9) "in order to prohibit domestic abusers convicted under run-of-the-mill misdemeanor assault and battery laws from possessing guns." Most states allow recklessness to prove assault.

Thomas, J., joined by Sotomayor, J., dissented on statutory interpretation grounds. In the portion of the dissent Sotomayor did not join, Thomas also argued that the majority read "the statute in a way that creates serious constitutional problems." The way the Court reads the statute, a "mother who slaps her 18-year-old son for talking back to her—an intentional use of force—could lose her right to bear arms forever if she is cited by the police under a local ordinance. The majority seeks to expand that already broad rule to any reckless physical injury or nonconsensual touch. I would not extend the statute into that constitutionally problematic territory."

CHAPTER 8

EQUAL PROTECTION

■ ■ ■

8–2 SUSPECT CLASSES AND OTHER CLASSIFICATIONS

8–2.1 RACE

8–2.14 Reverse Discrimination

8–2.14.1 Education

Unabridged, p. 770; add to end of *Notes*, to Note 6:

Abridged, p. 602; add to end of *Notes*, new Note 6:

Fisher v. University of Texas, 579 U.S. ___, 136 S.Ct. 2198, 195 L.Ed.2d 511 (2016)(4–3; Kagan, J., not participating). Kennedy, J., spoke for the Court. Plaintiff sued claiming that the University of Texas' "consideration of race as part of its holistic-review process disadvantaged her and other Caucasian applicants, in violation of the Equal Protection Clause." The University, following state law, offers to admit any student who graduates in the top 10% of a Texas high school. The University fills up the remaining spaces (about 25%) using a holistic review, counting various factors including race. It added this holistic review in response to *Gutter*, in an effort to admit more minority students than the top 10% plan admitted.

The Court approved this holistic admission, although it wrote the opinion narrowly. "The University's program is *sui generis*." Fisher did not challenge the top 10% plan, which "has been taken, somewhat artificially, as a given premise." Her decision not to challenge the top 10% plan "has led to a record that is almost devoid of information about the students who secured admission to the University through the Plan." Rather "than prolong a suit that has already persisted for eight years," the Court will decide and affirm the lower court. "The fact that this case has been litigated on a somewhat artificial basis, furthermore, may limit its value for prospective guidance." In addition, the University has a "continuing obligation to satisfy the burden of strict scrutiny in light of changing circumstances." In 2003, at the time of *Gutter*, 11% of Texas residents enrolled in the University were Hispanic and 3.5% were black; in 2007, 16.9% of the freshmen were Hispanic and 6.8% were black. The increases "show that consideration of race has had a meaningful, if still limited, effect on the diversity of the University's freshman class." Kennedy concluded by saying: "The Court's affirmance of the University's admissions policy today does not necessarily mean the University may rely on that same policy without refinement. It is the University's ongoing obligation to engage in constant deliberation and continued reflection regarding its admissions policies."

Alito, J., joined by Roberts, C.J., & Thomas, J., dissented. "[T]he majority notes that this litigation has persisted for many years, that petitioner has already graduated from another college, that UT's [University of Texas] policy may have changed over time, and that this case may offer little prospective guidance. At most, these considerations counsel in favor of dismissing this case as improvidently granted. . . . The majority cannot side with UT simply because it is tired of this case."

UT's consideration of race "pervades every aspect of UT's admissions process. See App. 219a ('We are certainly aware of the applicant's race. It's on the front page of the application that's being read [and] is used in context with everything else that's part of the applicant's file'). This is by design, as UT considers its use of racial classifications to be a benign form of 'social engineering.' " (Quoting Bill Powers, President of UT from 2006–2015). Alito also objected that UT provides no definition of the various ethnic groups. It "relies on applicants to 'classify themselves.' This is an invitation for applicants to game the system."

Alito added that UT admitted that "the [top 10%] percentage plan certainly helps with minority admissions, by and large," but UT argued it also needed its holistic review because it "needs race-conscious admissions in order to admit '[t]he African-American or Hispanic child of successful professionals in Dallas')." "Thus, the Top Ten Percent Law is faulted for admitting *the wrong kind of African-American and Hispanic students*." [Emphasis in original.] UT argues, "it needs affirmative action to admit privileged minorities."

Thomas, J., also dissented: "the Court's decision today is irreconcilable with strict scrutiny, rests on pernicious assumptions about race, and departs from many of our precedents."

8–3 FUNDAMENTAL RIGHTS

8–3.2 VOTING [UNABRIDGED]

8–3.1 VOTING [ABRIDGED]

8–3.21 Apportionment [Unabridged]

8–3.11 Apportionment [Abridged]

Unabridged, p. 853; add to end of *Notes*, new Note 7:

Abridged, p. 665; add to end of *Notes*, new Note 5:

Evenwel v. Abbott, 588 U.S.___, 136 S.Ct. 1120, 194 L.Ed.2d 291 (2016). Texas draws its legislative districts on the basis of total population, for one person, one vote. The maximum total-population deviation of the state senate districts was 8.04%, well within the presumptively permissible 10% range. However, if one looked at eligible-voter or registered-voter population, the map's maximum population deviation exceeds 40% because some areas had a disproportionate number of nonvoters, such as aliens. Plaintiffs argued that basing apportionment on total population dilutes their votes in relation to voters in other Senate districts, in violation of one person, one vote. Ginsburg, J., for the Court (with no dissents), rejected this argument: "We hold, based on constitutional history, this Court's decisions, and longstanding practice, that a State *may draw* its legislative districts based on total population." (Emphasis added.) The Court acknowledged that two state constitutions authorize the exclusion of noncitizen immigrants, and a few states exclude certain non-permanent residents, including nonresident members of the military. Still, "Adopting voter-eligible apportionment as constitutional command would upset a well-functioning approach to districting that all 50 States and countless local jurisdictions have followed for decades, even centuries." The Court added, "we need not and do not resolve whether, as Texas now argues, States may draw district to equalize voter-eligible population rather than total population."

Thomas, J., and Alito, J., each filed opinions concurring in the judgment. In part of the Alito opinion (which Thomas joined), Alito made clear that he rejected the Solicitor General's argument that states *must* use total population because the Constitution allocates House seats based on total population. "[E]ven the allocation of House seats does not comport with one person, one vote," because each state is entitled to at least one representative. One Representative in Wyoming represents fewer than 570,000 people while the one next door in Montana represents nearly a million. Alito concludes, this case only holds that "Texas permissibly used total population in drawing the challenged legislative districts."

8–3.4 PRIVACY AND SEXUAL AUTONOMY [UNABRIDGED]

8–3.3 PRIVACY AND SEXUAL AUTONOMY [ABRIDGED]

8–3.43 Abortion [Unabridged]

8–3.33 Abortion [Abridged]

Unabridged, p. 935; add to end of *Notes*, new Note 4:

Abridged, p. 728; add to end of *Notes*, new Note 4:

4. *Whole Woman's Health v. Hellerstedt*, 579 U.S.___, 136 S.Ct. 2293, 195 L.Ed.2d 665 (2016). Abortion providers sued Texas officials to enjoin them from implementing a statute (H.B. 2) that required abortion providers (1) to have admitting privileges at a local hospital located no more than 30 miles from their abortion facility and (2) to require that abortion facilities meet minimum standards in Texas for ambulatory surgical centers (ASCs). The trial court enjoined the law, but the Fifth Circuit reversed. The Supreme Court (5 to 3) reversed the Fifth Circuit and enjoined the law. This case is the first since 1992 that Justice Kennedy joined to invalidate a law regarding abortion as an "undue burden."

Breyer, J., for the Court, first rejected the procedural obstacles to the plaintiffs' case. Res judicata does not bar plaintiffs, even though many of the same plaintiffs earlier lost a lawsuit seeking to invalidate this same Texas law. In the earlier case involving the admitting privileges prong of H.B.2, "plaintiffs brought their facial challenge to the admitting-privileges requirement *prior to its enforcement*—before many abortion clinics had closed and while it was still unclear how many clinics would be affected. Here, petitioners bring an as-applied challenge to the requirement *after its enforcement*—and after a large number of clinics have in fact closed. The post enforcement consequences of H.B. 2 were unknowable before it went into effect." (Emphasis in original.) New evidence can give rise to a new claim.

In addition, there is no res judicata or issue preclusion to bar the challenge to the surgical care requirement because the plaintiffs in the earlier decision did not bring that claim, which is a separate and distinct provision of H.B. 2. Also, when the plaintiffs brought the earlier claim, the relevant Texas agency "had not yet issued" implementing regulations. "Finally, the relevant factual circumstances changed" since the earlier lower court decision.

The Court went on to hold that both provisions impose an "undue burden" on women seeking abortion. First, complications requiring hospital admissions occur in less than one-half of 1% of the cases. Once the hospital admitting requirement went into effect, the number of abortion facilities "dropped in half, from 40 to about 20," the "number of women of reproductive age living more than 50 miles from a clinic has doubled . . ." The surgical center requirement is also an undue burden. The trial court found that "risks are not appreciably lowered for patients who undergo abortions at ambulatory surgical centers as compared to nonsurgical-center facilities." Moreover, "the parties stipulated that the [ASC] requirement would further reduce the number of abortion facilities available to seven or eight facilities, located in Houston, Austin, San Antonio, and Dallas/Fort Worth." The Court concluded, "neither of these provisions confers medical benefits sufficient to justify the burdens upon access that each imposes. Each places a substantial obstacle in the path of women seeking a previability abortion, each constitutes an undue burden on abortion access, and each violates the Federal Constitution."

The Court said it was significant that "the relevant statute here does not set forth any legislative findings." Consequently, in examining the health benefits, it was proper for the district court, in the course of invalidating H.B. 2, to consider "the evidence in the record—including expert evidence, presented in stipulations, depositions, and testimony. It then weighed the asserted benefits against the burdens," and found that H.B. 2 imposed an undue burden.

The Court invalidated all of H.B. 2. It acknowledged, "The severability clause says that 'every provision, section, subsection, sentence, clause, phrase, or word in this Act, and every application of the provision in this Act, are severable from each other." Nonetheless, Breyer, for the Court, held that statute is not severable: "The provisions are unconstitutional on their face: Including a severability provision in the law does not change that conclusion." If such "a severability clause could impose such a [severability] requirement on courts, legislatures would easily be able to insulate unconstitutional statutes from most facial review."

Alito, J., joined by Roberts, C.J. & Thomas, J., dissented. He first focused on res judicata and issue preclusion:

> "[T]he Court's holding that petitioners' second facial challenge to the admitting privileges requirement is not barred by claim preclusion is not supported by any of our cases or any body of lower court precedent; is contrary to the bedrock rule that a party cannot relitigate a claim simply because the party has obtained new and better evidence; . . . In a regular case, an attempt by petitioners to relitigate their previously unsuccessful facial challenge to the admitting privileges requirement would have been rejected out of hand—indeed, might have resulted in the imposition of sanctions under Federal Rule of Civil Procedure 11. No court would even think of reviving such a claim on its own. But in this abortion case, ordinary rules of law—and fairness—are suspended."

On the merits, Alito said that the Court's conclusion that this law *caused* some abortion clinics to close "is belied by petitioners' own submissions to this Court." Petitioners "put on evidence of actual clinic capacity in their earlier case, and there is no apparent reason why they could not have done the same here." Instead, they just inferred that clinics closed because of H.B. 2.

H.B. 2 did cause *some* abortion clinics to close. After all, "H.B. 2 was intended to force unsafe facilities to shut down." Texas and other states enacted these restrictions "in the wake of the Kermit Gosnell scandal, in which a physician who ran an abortion clinic in Philadelphia was convicted for the first-degree murder of three infants who were born alive and for the manslaughter of a patient. Gosnell had not been actively supervised by state or local authorities or by his peers, and the Philadelphia grand jury that investigated the case recommended that the Commonwealth adopt a law requiring abortion clinics to comply with the same regulations as ASCs. If Pennsylvania had had such a requirement in force, the Gosnell facility may have been shut down before his crimes. And if there were any similarly unsafe facilities in Texas, H.B. 2 was clearly intended to put them out of business."

In answer to this argument, Breyer responded:

> "Gosnell, a physician in Pennsylvania, was convicted of first-degree murder and manslaughter. He 'staffed his facility with unlicensed and indifferent workers, and then let them practice medicine

unsupervised' and had '[d]irty facilities; unsanitary instruments; an absence of functioning monitoring and resuscitation equipment; the use of cheap, but dangerous, drugs; illegal procedures; and inadequate emergency access for when things inevitably went wrong.' Gosnell's behavior was terribly wrong. But there is no reason to believe that an extra layer of regulation would have affected that behavior. Determined wrongdoers, already ignoring existing statutes and safety measures, are unlikely to be convinced to adopt safe practices by a new overlay of regulations. Regardless, Gosnell's deplorable crimes could escape detection only because his facility went uninspected for more than 15 years."

Alito also objected to Breyer's severability argument:

"By forgoing severability, the Court strikes down numerous provisions that could not plausibly impose an undue burden. For example, surgical center patients must 'be treated with respect, consideration, and dignity.' That's now enjoined. Patients may not be given misleading 'advertising regarding the competence and/or capabilities of the organization.' Enjoined. Centers must maintain fire alarm and emergency communications systems, and eliminate '[h]azards that might lead to slipping, falling, electrical shock, burns, poisoning, or other trauma.' Enjoined and enjoined."

Thomas, J., also filed a separate dissent to "to emphasize how today's decision perpetuates the Court's habit of applying different rules to different constitutional rights—especially the putative right to abortion."

8–3.44 Homosexuality [Unabridged]

8–3.34 Homosexuality [Abridged]

Unabridged, p. 959; add end of section:

Abridged, p. 751; add end of section:

OBERGEFELL V. HODGES

576 U.S. ___, 135 S.Ct. 2584, 192 L.Ed.2d 609 (2015).

JUSTICE KENNEDY delivered the opinion of the Court.

The Constitution promises liberty to all within its reach, a liberty that includes certain specific rights that allow persons, within a lawful realm, to define and express their identity. The petitioners in these cases seek to find that liberty by marrying someone of the same sex and having their marriages deemed lawful on the same terms and conditions as marriages between persons of the opposite sex.

These cases come from Michigan, Kentucky, Ohio, and Tennessee, States that define marriage as a union between one man and one woman. . . . The Court of Appeals held that a State has no constitutional obligation to license same-sex marriages or to recognize same-sex marriages performed out of State. . . . This Court granted review, limited to two questions. The first, presented by the cases from Michigan and Kentucky, is whether the Fourteenth Amendment requires a State to license a marriage between two people of the same sex. The second, presented by the cases from Ohio, Tennessee, and, again, Kentucky, is whether the Fourteenth Amendment requires a State to recognize a same-sex marriage licensed and performed in a State which does grant that right. . . .

From their beginning to their most recent page, the annals of human history reveal the transcendent importance of marriage. The lifelong union of a man and a woman always has promised nobility and dignity to all persons, without regard to their station in life. Marriage is sacred to those who live by their religions and offers unique fulfillment to those who find meaning in the secular realm. . . .

The centrality of marriage to the human condition makes it unsurprising that the institution has existed for millennia and across civilizations. Since the dawn of history, marriage has transformed strangers into relatives, binding families and societies together. Confucius taught that marriage lies at the foundation of government. This wisdom was echoed centuries later and half a world away by Cicero, who wrote, "The first bond of society is marriage; next, children; and then the family." There are untold references to the beauty of marriage in religious and philosophical texts spanning time, cultures, and faiths, as well as in art and literature in all their forms. It is fair and necessary to say these references were based on the understanding that marriage is a union between two persons of the opposite sex.

That history is the beginning of these cases. The respondents say it should be the end as well. To them, it would demean a timeless institution if the concept and lawful status of marriage were extended to two persons of the same sex. Marriage, in their view, is by its nature a gender-differentiated union of man and woman. This view long has been held—and continues to be held—in good faith by reasonable and sincere people here and throughout the world.

The petitioners acknowledge this history but contend that these cases cannot end there. . . . Far from seeking to devalue marriage, the petitioners seek it for themselves because of their respect—and need—for its privileges and responsibilities. And their immutable nature dictates that same-sex marriage is their only real path to this profound commitment. . . .

The ancient origins of marriage confirm its centrality, but it has not stood in isolation from developments in law and society. The history of marriage is one of both continuity and change. That institution—even as confined to opposite-sex relations—has evolved over time. . . .

This Court first gave detailed consideration to the legal status of homosexuals in *Bowers* v. *Hardwick*, 478 U.S. 186 (1986). There it upheld the constitutionality of a Georgia law deemed to criminalize certain homosexual acts. Ten years later, in *Romer* v. *Evans*, 517 U.S. 620 (1996), the Court invalidated an amendment to Colorado's Constitution that sought to foreclose any branch or political subdivision of the State from protecting persons against discrimination based on sexual orientation. Then, in 2003, the Court overruled *Bowers*, holding that laws making same-sex intimacy a crime "demea[n] the lives of homosexual persons." *Lawrence* v. *Texas*, 539 U.S. 558, 575. . . .

The nature of injustice is that we may not always see it in our own times. The generations that wrote and ratified the Bill of Rights and the Fourteenth Amendment did not presume to know the extent of freedom in all of its dimensions, and so they entrusted to future generations a charter protecting the right of all persons to enjoy liberty as we learn its meaning. When new insight reveals discord between the Constitution's central protections and a received legal stricture, a claim to liberty must be addressed.

Applying these established tenets, the Court has long held the right to marry is protected by the Constitution. In *Loving* v. *Virginia*, 388 U.S. 1, 12 (1967), which invalidated bans on interracial unions, a unanimous Court held marriage is "one of the vital personal rights essential to the orderly pursuit of happiness by free men." The Court reaffirmed that holding in *Zablocki* v. *Redhail*, 434 U.S. 374, 384 (1978), which held the right to marry was burdened by a law prohibiting fathers who were behind on child support from marrying. The Court again applied this principle in *Turner* v. *Safley*, 482 U.S. 78, 95 (1987), which held the right to marry was abridged by regulations limiting the privilege of prison inmates to marry. Over time and in other contexts, the Court has reiterated that the right to marry is fundamental under the Due Process Clause. *Griswold*, *supra*, *Skinner* v. *Oklahoma ex rel. Williamson*, 316 U.S. 535, 541 (1942).

[T]his Court's cases describing the right to marry presumed a relationship involving opposite-sex partners. The Court, like many institutions, has made assumptions defined by the world and time of which it is a part. This was evident in *Baker* v. *Nelson*, 409 U.S. 810, a one-line summary decision issued in 1972, holding the exclusion of same-sex couples from marriage did not present a substantial federal question.

Still, there are other, more instructive precedents. This Court's cases have expressed constitutional principles of broader reach. In defining the right to marry these cases have identified essential attributes of that right based in history, tradition, and other constitutional liberties inherent in this intimate bond. [I]n assessing whether the force and rationale of its cases apply to same-sex couples, the Court must respect the basic reasons why the right to marry has been long protected.

This analysis compels the conclusion that same-sex couples may exercise the right to marry. The four principles and traditions to be discussed demonstrate that the reasons marriage is fundamental under the Constitution apply with equal force to same-sex couples.

A first premise of the Court's relevant precedents is that the right to personal choice regarding marriage is inherent in the concept of individual autonomy. This abiding connection between marriage and liberty is why *Loving* invalidated interracial marriage bans under the Due Process Clause. . . . The nature of marriage is that, through its enduring bond, two persons together can find other freedoms, such as expression, intimacy, and spirituality. . . .

A second principle in this Court's jurisprudence is that the right to marry is fundamental because it supports a two-person union unlike any other in its importance to the committed individuals. This point was central to *Griswold* v. *Connecticut*, which held the Constitution protects the right of married couples to use contraception. . . .

A third basis for protecting the right to marry is that it safeguards children and families and thus draws meaning from related rights of childrearing, procreation, and education. [M]any same-sex couples provide loving and nurturing homes to their children, whether biological or adopted. . . . Excluding same-sex couples from marriage thus conflicts with a central premise of the right to marry. Without the recognition, stability, and predictability marriage offers, their children suffer the stigma of knowing their families are somehow lesser. They also suffer the significant material costs of being raised by unmarried parents, relegated through no fault of their own to a more difficult and uncertain family life. The marriage laws at issue here thus harm and humiliate the children of same-sex couples.

That is not to say the right to marry is less meaningful for those who do not or cannot have children. An ability, desire, or promise to procreate is not and has not been a prerequisite for a valid marriage in any State. In light of precedent protecting the right of a married couple not to procreate, it cannot be said the Court or the States have conditioned the right to marry on the capacity or commitment to procreate. The constitutional marriage right has many aspects, of which childbearing is only one.

Fourth and finally, this Court's cases and the Nation's traditions make clear that marriage is a keystone of our social order. [J]ust as a couple vows to support each other, so does society pledge to support the couple, offering symbolic recognition and material benefits to protect and nourish the union. Indeed, while the States are in general free to vary the benefits they confer on all married couples, they have throughout our history made marriage the basis for an expanding list of governmental rights, benefits, and responsibilities. These aspects of marital status include: taxation; inheritance and property rights; rules of intestate succession; spousal privilege in the law of evidence; hospital access; medical decision making authority; adoption rights; the rights and benefits of survivors; birth and death certificates; professional ethics rules; campaign finance restrictions; workers' compensation benefits; health insurance; and child custody, support, and visitation rules. [B]y virtue of their exclusion from that institution, same-sex couples are denied the constellation of benefits that the States have linked to marriage. This harm results in more than just material burdens. . . . It demeans gays and lesbians for the State to lock them out of a central institution of the Nation's society. Same-sex couples, too, may aspire to the transcendent purposes of marriage and seek fulfillment in its highest meaning.

The limitation of marriage to opposite-sex couples may long have seemed natural and just, but its inconsistency with the central meaning of the fundamental right to marry is now manifest. With that knowledge must come the recognition that laws excluding same-sex couples from the marriage right impose stigma and injury of the kind prohibited by our basic charter.

. . . Many who deem same-sex marriage to be wrong reach that conclusion based on decent and honorable religious or philosophical premises, and neither they nor their beliefs are disparaged here. But when that sincere, personal opposition becomes enacted law and public policy, the necessary consequence is to put the imprimatur of the State itself on an exclusion that soon demeans or stigmatizes those whose own liberty is then denied. Under the Constitution, same-sex couples seek in marriage the same legal treatment as opposite-sex couples, and it would disparage their choices and diminish their personhood to deny them this right.

The right of same-sex couples to marry that is part of the liberty promised by the Fourteenth Amendment is derived, too, from that Amendment's guarantee of the equal protection of the laws. The Due Process Clause and the Equal Protection Clause are connected in a profound way, though they set forth independent principles. Rights implicit in liberty and rights secured by equal protection may rest on different precepts and are not always co-extensive, yet in some instances each may be instructive as to the meaning and reach of the other. [T]he right to marry is a fundamental right inherent in the liberty of the person, and under the Due Process and Equal Protection Clauses of the Fourteenth Amendment couples of the same-sex may not be deprived of that right and that liberty. The Court now holds that same-sex couples may exercise the fundamental right to marry. No longer may this liberty be denied to them. *Baker* v. *Nelson* must be and now is overruled, and the State laws challenged by Petitioners in these cases are now held invalid to the extent they exclude same-sex couples from civil marriage on the same terms and conditions as opposite-sex couples.

There may be an initial inclination in these cases to proceed with caution—to await further legislation, litigation, and debate. . . . Yet there has been far more deliberation than this argument acknowledges. There have been referenda, legislative debates, and grassroots campaigns, as well as countless studies, papers, books, . . . extensive litigation in state and federal courts . . . more than 100 *amici* [briefs].

[T]he Constitution contemplates that democracy is the appropriate process for change, so long as that process does not abridge fundamental rights. . . . The dynamic of our constitutional system is that individuals need not await legislative action before asserting a fundamental right. The Nation's courts are open to injured individuals who come to them to vindicate their own direct, personal stake in our basic charter. An individual can invoke a right to constitutional protection when he or she is harmed, even if the broader public disagrees and even if the legislature refuses to act. . . .

Finally, it must be emphasized that religions, and those who adhere to religious doctrines, may continue to advocate with utmost, sincere conviction that, by divine precepts, same-sex marriage should not be condoned. The First Amendment ensures that religious organizations and persons are given proper protection as they seek to teach the principles that are so fulfilling and so central to their lives and faiths, and to their own deep aspirations to continue the family structure they have long revered. The same is true of those who oppose same-sex marriage for other reasons. In turn, those who believe allowing same-sex marriage is proper or indeed essential, whether as a matter of religious conviction or secular belief, may engage those who disagree with their view in an open and searching debate. The Constitution, however, does not permit the State to bar same-sex couples from marriage on the same terms as accorded to couples of the opposite sex.

. . . Leaving the current state of affairs in place would maintain and promote instability and uncertainty. For some couples, even an ordinary drive into a neighboring State to visit family or friends risks causing severe hardship in the event of a spouse's hospitalization while across state lines. In light of the fact that many States already allow same-sex marriage—and hundreds of thousands of these marriages already have occurred—the disruption caused by the recognition bans is significant and ever-growing. . . . The Court, in this decision, holds same-sex couples may exercise the fundamental right to marry in all States. It follows that . . . there is no lawful basis for a State to refuse to recognize a lawful same-sex marriage performed in another State on the ground of its same-sex character. . . . The judgment of the Court of Appeals for the Sixth Circuit is reversed. It is so ordered.

CHIEF JUSTICE ROBERTS, with whom JUSTICE SCALIA and JUSTICE THOMAS join, dissenting.

[T]his Court is not a legislature. Whether same-sex marriage is a good idea should be of no concern to us. Under the Constitution, judges have power to say what the law is, not what it should be. The people who ratified the Constitution authorized courts to exercise "neither force nor will but merely judgment." The Federalist No. 78.

Although the policy arguments for extending marriage to same-sex couples may be compelling, the legal arguments for requiring such an extension are not. The fundamental right to marry does not include a right to make a State change its definition of marriage. And a State's decision to maintain the meaning of marriage that has persisted in every culture throughout human history can hardly be called irrational. In short, our Constitution does not enact any one theory of marriage. The people of a State are free to expand marriage to include same-sex couples, or to retain the historic definition.

Today, however, the Court takes the extraordinary step of ordering every State to license and recognize same-sex marriage. Many people will rejoice at this decision, and I begrudge none their celebration. But for those who believe in a government of laws, not of men, the majority's approach is deeply disheartening. Supporters of same-sex marriage have achieved considerable success persuading their fellow citizens—through the democratic process—to adopt their view. That ends today. Five lawyers have closed the debate and enacted their own vision of marriage as a matter of constitutional law. Stealing this issue from the people will for many cast a cloud over same-sex marriage, making a dramatic social change that much more difficult to accept. [T]he Court invalidates the marriage laws of more than half the States and orders the transformation of a social institution that has formed the basis of human society for millennia, for the Kalahari Bushmen and the Han Chinese, the Carthaginians and the Aztecs. Just who do we think we are? . . .

Petitioners and their *amici* base their arguments on the "right to marry" and the imperative of "marriage equality." There is no serious dispute that, under our precedents, the Constitution protects a right to marry and requires States to apply their marriage laws equally. The real question in these cases is what constitutes "marriage," or—more precisely—*who decides* what constitutes "marriage"? [T]he majority acknowledges, marriage "has existed for millennia and across civilizations." For all those millennia, across all those civilizations, "marriage" referred to only one relationship: the union of a man and a woman. Tr. of Oral Arg. (petitioners conceding that they are not aware of any society that permitted same-sex marriage before 2001). . . . Marriage did not come about as a result of a political movement, discovery, disease, war, religious doctrine, or any other moving force of world history—and certainly not as a result of a prehistoric decision to exclude gays and lesbians. It arose in the nature of things to meet a vital need: ensuring that children are conceived by a mother and father committed to raising them in the stable conditions of a lifelong relationship. [F]or the good of children and society, sexual relations that can lead to procreation should occur only between a man and a woman committed to a lasting bond. Society has recognized that bond as marriage. And by bestowing a respected status and material benefits on married couples, society encourages men and women to conduct sexual relations within marriage rather than without. As one prominent scholar put it, "Marriage is a socially arranged solution for the problem of getting people to stay together and care for children that the mere desire for children, and the sex that makes children possible, does not solve." J. Q. Wilson, The Marriage Problem 41 (2002).

This singular understanding of marriage has prevailed in the United States throughout our history. . . . The Constitution itself says nothing about marriage, and the Framers thereby entrusted the States with "[t]he whole subject of the domestic relations of husband and wife." *Windsor*. There is no dispute that every State at the founding—and every State throughout our history until a dozen years ago—defined marriage in the traditional, biologically rooted way. . . .

Petitioners first contend that the marriage laws of their States violate the Due Process Clause. The Solicitor General of the United States, appearing in support of petitioners, expressly disowned that position before this Court. The majority nevertheless resolves these cases for petitioners based almost entirely on the Due Process Clause.

[T]he majority's approach has no basis in principle or tradition, except for the unprincipled tradition of judicial policymaking that characterized discredited decisions such as *Lochner* v. *New York*, 198 U.S. 45. Stripped of its shiny rhetorical gloss, the majority's argument is that the Due Process Clause gives same-sex couples a fundamental right to marry because it will be good for them and for society. If I were a legislator, I would certainly consider that view as a matter of social policy. But as a judge, I find the majority's position indefensible as a matter of constitutional law. . . .

Allowing unelected federal judges to select which unenumerated rights rank as "fundamental"—and to strike down state laws on the basis of that determination—raises obvious concerns about the judicial role. . . . One immediate question invited by the majority's position is whether States may retain the definition of marriage as a union of two people. Cf. *Brown* v. *Buhman*, 947 F. Supp. 2d 1170 (Utah 2013), appeal pending, No. 14–

4117 (CA10). Although the majority randomly inserts the adjective "two" in various places, it offers no reason at all why the two-person element of the core definition of marriage may be preserved while the man-woman element may not. Indeed, from the standpoint of history and tradition, a leap from opposite-sex marriage to same-sex marriage is much greater than one from a two-person union to plural unions, which have deep roots in some cultures around the world. If the majority is willing to take the big leap, it is hard to see how it can say no to the shorter one.

It is striking how much of the majority's reasoning would apply with equal force to the claim of a fundamental right to plural marriage. If "[t]here is dignity in the bond between two men or two women who seek to marry and in their autonomy to make such profound choices," why would there be any less dignity in the bond between three people who, in exercising their autonomy, seek to make the profound choice to marry? If a same-sex couple has the constitutional right to marry because their children would otherwise "suffer the stigma of knowing their families are somehow lesser," why wouldn't the same reasoning apply to a family of three or more persons raising children? If not having the opportunity to marry "serves to disrespect and subordinate" gay and lesbian couples, why wouldn't the same "imposition of this disability," serve to disrespect and subordinate people who find fulfillment in polyamorous relationships? See Bennett, Polyamory: The Next Sexual Revolution? Newsweek, July 28, 2009 (estimating 500,000 polyamorous families in the United States); Li, Married Lesbian "Throuple" Expecting First Child, N. Y. Post, Apr. 23, 2014; Otter, Three May Not Be a Crowd: The Case for a Constitutional Right to Plural Marriage, 64 Emory L. J. 1977 (2015).

Nowhere is the majority's extravagant conception of judicial supremacy more evident than in its description—and dismissal—of the public debate regarding same-sex marriage. Yes, the majority concedes, on one side are thousands of years of human history in every society known to have populated the planet. But on the other side, there has been "extensive litigation," "many thoughtful District Court decisions," "countless studies, papers, books, and other popular and scholarly writings," and "more than 100" *amicus* briefs in these cases alone. What would be the point of allowing the democratic process to go on? It is high time for the Court to decide the meaning of marriage, based on five lawyers' "better informed understanding" of "a liberty that remains urgent in our own era." The answer is surely there in one of those *amicus* briefs or studies.

Those who founded our country would not recognize the majority's conception of the judicial role. They after all risked their lives and fortunes for the precious right to govern themselves. [P]eople are in the midst of a serious and thoughtful public debate on the issue of same-sex marriage. They see voters carefully considering same-sex marriage, casting ballots in favor or opposed, and sometimes changing their minds. They see political leaders similarly reexamining their positions, and either reversing course or explaining adherence to old convictions confirmed anew. They see governments and businesses modifying policies and practices with respect to same-sex couples, and participating actively in the civic discourse. They see countries overseas democratically accepting profound social change, or declining to do so. This deliberative process is making people take seriously questions that they may not have even regarded as questions before. . . .

Respect for sincere religious conviction has led voters and legislators in every State that has adopted same-sex marriage democratically to include accommodations for religious practice. The majority's decision imposing same-sex marriage cannot, of course, create any such accommodations. The majority graciously suggests that religious believers may continue to "advocate" and "teach" their views of marriage. The First Amendment guarantees, however, the freedom to "*exercise*" religion. Ominously, that is not a word the majority uses. . . .

JUSTICE SCALIA, with whom JUSTICE THOMAS joins, dissenting.

. . . . Today's decree says that my Ruler, and the Ruler of 320 million Americans coast-to-coast, is a majority of the nine lawyers on the Supreme Court. The opinion in these cases is the furthest extension in fact—and the furthest extension one can even imagine—of the Court's claimed power to create "liberties" that the Constitution and its Amendments neglect to mention. This practice of constitutional revision by an unelected committee of nine, always accompanied (as it is today) by extravagant praise of liberty, robs the People of the most important liberty they asserted in the Declaration of Independence and won in the Revolution of 1776: the freedom to govern themselves. [E]lectorates of 11 States, either directly or through their representatives, chose to expand the traditional definition of marriage. Many more decided not to. Win or lose, advocates for both sides continued pressing their cases, secure in the knowledge that an electoral loss can be negated by a later electoral win. That is exactly how our system of government is supposed to work.

[T]he Court ends this debate, in an opinion lacking even a thin veneer of law. Buried beneath the mummeries and straining-to-be-memorable passages of the opinion is a candid and startling assertion: No matter *what* it was the People ratified, the Fourteenth Amendment protects those rights that the Judiciary, in its "reasoned judgment," thinks the Fourteenth Amendment ought to protect. That is so because "[t]he generations that wrote and ratified the Bill of Rights and the Fourteenth Amendment did not presume to know the extent of freedom in all of its dimensions . . ." One would think that sentence would continue: ". . . and therefore they provided for a means by which the People could amend the Constitution," or perhaps ". . . and therefore they left the creation of additional liberties, such as the freedom to marry someone of the same sex, to the People, through the never-ending process of legislation." But no. What logically follows, in the majority's judge-empowering estimation, is: "and so they entrusted to future generations a charter protecting the right of all persons to enjoy liberty as we learn its meaning." The "we," needless to say, is the nine of us. . . .

Judges are selected precisely for their skill as lawyers; whether they reflect the policy views of a particular constituency is not (or should not be) relevant. Not surprisingly then, the Federal Judiciary is hardly a cross-section of America. Take, for example, this Court, which consists of only nine men and women, all of them successful lawyers who studied at Harvard or Yale Law School. Four of the nine are natives of New York City. Eight of them grew up in east- and west-coast States. Only one hails from the vast expanse in-between. Not a single Southwesterner or even, to tell the truth, a genuine Westerner (California does not count). Not a single evangelical Christian (a group that comprises about one quarter of Americans), or even a Protestant of any denomination. The strikingly unrepresentative character of the body voting on today's social upheaval would be irrelevant if they were functioning as *judges*, answering the legal question whether the American people had ever ratified a constitutional provision that was understood to proscribe the traditional definition of marriage. [T]o allow the policy question of same-sex marriage to be considered and resolved by a select, patrician, highly unrepresentative panel of nine is to violate a principle even more fundamental than no taxation without representation: no social transformation without representation.

But what really astounds is the hubris reflected in today's judicial Putsch. The five Justices who compose today's majority are entirely comfortable concluding that every State violated the Constitution for all of the 135 years between the Fourteenth Amendment's ratification and Massachusetts' permitting of same-sex marriages in 2003.

[The Court's] opinion is couched in a style that is as pretentious as its content is egotistic. It is one thing for separate concurring or dissenting opinions to contain extravagances, even silly extravagances, of thought and expression; it is something else for the official opinion of the Court to do so.[22] Of course the opinion's showy profundities are often profoundly incoherent. "The nature of marriage is that, through its enduring bond, two persons together can find other freedoms, such as expression, intimacy, and spirituality." (Really? Who ever thought that intimacy and spirituality [whatever that means] were freedoms? And if intimacy is, one would think

[22] If, even as the price to be paid for a fifth vote, I ever joined an opinion for the Court that began: "The Constitution promises liberty to all within its reach, a liberty that includes certain specific rights that allow persons, within a lawful realm, to define and express their identity," I would hide my head in a bag. The Supreme Court of the United States has descended from the disciplined legal reasoning of John Marshall and Joseph Story to the mystical aphorisms of the fortune cookie.

Freedom of Intimacy is abridged rather than expanded by marriage. Ask the nearest hippie. Expression, sure enough, *is* a freedom, but anyone in a long-lasting marriage will attest that that happy state constricts, rather than expands, what one can prudently say.) . . .

JUSTICE THOMAS, with whom JUSTICE SCALIA joins, dissenting. . . .

Numerous *amici*—even some not supporting the States—have cautioned the Court that its decision here will "have unavoidable and wide-ranging implications for religious liberty." In our society, marriage is not simply a governmental institution; it is a religious institution as well. Today's decision might change the former, but it cannot change the latter. [T]he two will come into conflict, particularly as individuals and churches are confronted with demands to participate in and endorse civil marriages between same-sex couples. . . . Religious liberty is about freedom of action in matters of religion generally, and the scope of that liberty is directly correlated to the civil restraints placed upon religious practice. . . .

JUSTICE ALITO, with whom JUSTICE SCALIA and JUSTICE THOMAS join, dissenting. . . .

Today's decision usurps the constitutional right of the people to decide whether to keep or alter the traditional understanding of marriage. [It also] will be used to vilify Americans who are unwilling to assent to the new orthodoxy. [T]he majority attempts, toward the end of its opinion, to reassure those who oppose same-sex marriage that their rights of conscience will be protected. We will soon see whether this proves to be true. I assume that those who cling to old beliefs will be able to whisper their thoughts in the recesses of their homes, but if they repeat those views in public, they will risk being labeled as bigots and treated as such by governments, employers, and schools. . . . Recalling the harsh treatment of gays and lesbians in the past, some may think that turnabout is fair play. But if that sentiment prevails, the Nation will experience bitter and lasting wounds. . . . Most Americans—understandably—will cheer or lament today's decision [b]ut all Americans, whatever their thinking on that issue, should worry about what the majority's claim of power portends.

NOTES

1. The majority never says that sexual orientation is a suspect class, subject to strict scrutiny. Is sexual orientation now a suspect class?

Runyon v. McCrary, 427 U.S. 160 (1976) [Casebook, § 9–2], held a federal law, 42 U.S.C.A § 1981, forbids racial discrimination in making private contracts. It also specifically said that it was not interpreting that statute to apply to private schools "that practice racial exclusion on religious grounds." *Heart of Atlanta Motel, Inc. v. United States*, 379 U.S. 241 (1964) [Casebook § 4–4], upheld federal commerce power to prohibit racial discrimination in places of public accommodation, and noted that law exempted landlords who lived in the building and offered "not more than five rooms for rent." This statutory exemption exists to this day. In *Hurley v. Irish-American Gay, Lesbian and Bisexual Group of Boston*, 515 U.S. 557 (1995) [Casebook unabridged, § 10–9.4, abridged], § 10–9.2, gay, lesbian, and bisexual descendants of Irish immigrants sought to march as a group in the St. Patrick's Day parade. The parade's private organizers refused and the state supreme court held that this exclusion violated Massachusetts' public accommodation law, which prohibits discrimination on account of, inter alia, sexual orientation, in places of public accommodation. Souter, J, for a unanimous Court, held that when Massachusetts required the defendants to alter the expressive content of their parade, it violated the First Amendment.

Should such cases apply to individuals who (on free speech or free exercise grounds) do not want to participate in gay marriages? For example, the state could provide that the baker cannot refuse to sell a cupcake to a customer because the customer is gay. [The parade organizers in *Hurley* did not exclude gays as individuals; they did exclude a gay pride float.] However, the baker may argue that creating a wedding cake (unlike selling a cupcake) is a work of art and participating in the wedding, thus a part of free speech. Is participating (or refusing to participate) in a wedding part of free expression, like a parade that excludes a gay pride float?

Consider wedding photographers. Taking a passport photo is not participating in the travel and it is not a work of art. Is taking a portfolio of wedding photos part of free expression? Could the photographer say, "I will not participate in your wedding by taking photographs because I do not believe in gay weddings"? Is that different from saying, "I will not participate in your wedding by taking photographs because you cuckolded me and now you are marrying my ex-wife"? Could the state force the cuckolded photographer to take the wedding photos? Or, "I will not participate in your wedding by taking photographs because you ran over my neighbor's dog 10 years ago"? May the state force the local baker to cater to a KKK rally? Could it force the gay baker to design and make a cake that says, "same sex marriage is morally wrong"?

Does it matter, in deciding these issues, whether or not *Obergefell* held that sexual orientation is a suspect class?

2. Justice Ginsburg, while on the D.C. Circuit, wrote a law review article arguing that *Roe v. Wade*, 410 U.S. 113 (1973), Casebook, unabridged, § 8–3.43; abridged, § 8–3.33, would have been more acceptable if the Court had not gone beyond a narrow ruling invalidating the particular statute in the case. "The political process was moving . . . , not swiftly enough for advocates of quick, complete change, but majoritarian institutions were listening and acting. Heavy-handed judicial intervention was difficult to justify and appears to have provoked, not resolved, conflict." Ginsburg, *Some Thoughts on Autonomy and Equality in Relation to Roe v. Wade*, 63 N. C. L. Rev. 375, 385–86 (1985) (footnote omitted). Should that argument apply to this case?

3. Chief Justice Roberts' dissent cites *Brown v. Buhman*, 947 F. Supp. 2d 1170 (Utah 2013), vacated as moot, 822 F.3d 1151 (10th Cir. May 13,

2016)(county attorney's announcement of policy limiting bigamy prosecutions rendered case moot). In that case, a polygamist family challenged the constitutionality of Utah's bigamy statute. The district court held that the cohabitation prong of the statute was "unconstitutional on numerous grounds and strikes it." The court allowed the statute "to remain in force as prohibiting bigamy in the literal sense—the fraudulent or otherwise impermissible possession of two purportedly valid marriage licenses for the purpose of entering into more than one purportedly legal marriage." The TV reality series, *Sister Wives*, featured the plaintiffs, Kody Brown, his four wives, and 17 children. The 10th Circuit dismissed the appeal as moot.

4. *Pavan v. Smith*, 582 U.S. ___, 137 S.Ct. 2075, ___L.Ed.2d ___, 2017 WL 2722472 (2017)(per curiam), summarily reversed the Arkansas Supreme Court and held that an Arkansas' birth certificate scheme violates *Obergefell.* Two married same-sex couples conceived children through anonymous sperm donation. An Arkansas statute generally required the name of mother's male spouse to appear on child's birth certificate when mother conceived a child by means of artificial insemination but it allowed omission of mother's female spouse from her child's birth certificate. Plaintiffs sued, arguing that this legislative scheme violated the Constitution

The divided Arkansas Supreme Court upheld the scheme arguing, "the statute centers on the relationship of the biological mother and the biological father to the child, not on the marital relationship of husband and wife," and "does not run afoul of *Obergefell.*" The Court rejected that argument. "[S]tate law, as interpreted by the court below, allows Arkansas officials in those very same circumstances to omit a married woman's female spouse from her child's birth certificate." "*Obergefell* proscribes such disparate treatment."

Gorsuch, J., joined by Thomas & Alito, JJ., dissented, arguing that summary reversal was an inappropriate way to decide that a state "birth registration scheme based on biology" violates *Obergefell.* Particularly where, as here, "the State has repeatedly conceded that the benefits afforded nonbiological parents under § 9–10–201 must be afforded equally to both same-sex and opposite-sex couples."

CHAPTER 10

FREEDOM OF SPEECH

■ ■ ■

10–3 TIME, PLACE, AND MANNER RESTRICTIONS AND THE PUBLIC FORUM

10–3.3 DEFINING THE PUBLIC FORUM [UNABRIDGED]

10–3.2 DEFINING THE PUBLIC FORUM [ABRIDGED]

Unabridged, p. 1076; add to *Notes*, add to end of Note 1:

Abridged, p. 839; add to *Notes*, add to end of Note 1:

Reed v. Town of Gilbert, 576 U.S.___, 135 S.Ct. 2218, 192 L.Ed.2d 236 (2015). Thomas, J., for the Court, reversed the 9th Circuit. There were no dissents. Town of Gilbert's sign ordinance is an unconstitutional, content-based regulation of speech. The town has a comprehensive sign code prohibiting the display of outdoor signs without a permit. It includes 23 exemptions, three of which apply to ideological, political, and temporary directional signs. While all three exemptions include various restrictions on size and/or time and placement, the temporary directional signs have greater restrictions than either ideological or political signs. The Good News Community Church holds services at different facilities because it does not have a permanent church. It uses temporary directional signs to invite people to services. The law provides that these signs may not be bigger than 6 square feet and can go up only 12 hours before their Sunday services start, which means that the church cannot post the signs until late on Saturday night when they are harder to see in the dark. The restrictions "depend entirely on the communicative content of the sign." For example, the Town treats differently a sign informing its reader of the time and place that a book club will discuss John Locke's Two Treatises of Government from a sign expressing the view that one should vote for one of Locke's followers in an upcoming election. "More to the point, the Church's signs inviting people to attend its worship services are treated differently from signs conveying other types of ideas. On its face, the Sign Code is a content-based regulation of speech." Placing strict limits on temporary directional signs is hardly necessary to beautify the Town when other types of signs create the same problem. Nor has the Town shown that temporary directional signs pose a greater threat to public safety than ideological or political signs.

The Town has ample "content-neutral options" available to resolve problems with safety and aesthetics, such as size, building materials, lighting, moving parts, and portability. The Town can also forbid posting signs on public property, so long as it does so in an evenhanded, content-neutral manner.

Unabridged, p. 1078; add to end of *Notes*, new Note 6:

Abridged, p. 840; add to end of *Notes*, new Note 4:

THE INTERNET. *Packingham v. North Carolina*, 582 U.S. ___, 137 S.Ct. 1730, 198 L.Ed.2d 273 (2017). A North Carolina statute makes it a felony for a registered sex offender "to access a commercial social networking Web site where the sex offender knows that the site permits minor children to become members or to create or maintain personal Web pages." Packingham was convicted of posting a statement on his personal Facebook profile about a positive experience in traffic court. The trial court gave him a suspended sentence.

Kennedy, J., (joined by Ginsburg, Breyer, Sotomayor, and Kagan; Gorsuch did not participate), held that North Carolina's law violates free speech clause. He cautioned, "The forces and directions of the Internet are so new, so protean, and so far reaching that courts must be conscious that what they say today might be obsolete tomorrow." Hence, "the Court must exercise extreme caution before suggesting that the First Amendment provides scant protection for access to vast networks in that medium."

Even if that this law is content neutral and subject to intermediate scrutiny, it is not narrowly tailored to serve a significant governmental interest. It applies to social networking sites like Facebook, LinkedIn, and Twitter. The Court assumed that, under the First Amendment, a state may enact specific, narrowly-tailored laws that prohibit a sex offender from engaging in conduct that often presages a sexual crime, like contacting a minor or using a website to gather information about a minor. The problem is that North Carolina prohibited much more, and could not show that its "sweeping law" was necessary to keep sex offenders away from minors:

> "North Carolina with one broad stroke bars access to what for many are the principal sources for knowing current events, checking ads for employment, speaking and listening in the modern public square, and otherwise exploring the vast realms of human thought and knowledge. These websites can provide perhaps the most powerful mechanisms available to a private citizen to make his or her voice heard. They allow a person with an Internet connection to 'become a town crier with a voice that resonates farther than it could from any soapbox.' "

Alito, J., concurred in the judgment, joined by Roberts, C.J., and Thomas, J., criticizing the majority for its "undisciplined dicta," and its inability "to resist musings that seem to equate the entirety of the internet with public streets and parks."

10–3.4 GOVERNMENT SUBSIDIZATION OF SPEECH [UNABRIDGED]

10–3.3 GOVERNMENT SUBSIDIZATION OF SPEECH [ABRIDGED]

Unabridged, p. 1085; add to *Notes*, new Note 3:

Abridged, p. 847; add to *Notes*, new Note 2:

Walker v. Texas Division, Sons of Confederate Veterans, Inc., 576 U.S. ___, 135 S.Ct. 2239, 192 L.Ed.2d 274 (2015). Texas allows automobile owners to choose a general-issue license plate or a specialty license plate (at an additional fee). The Confederate Veterans sued because Texas rejected a proposed specialty license plate design featuring a Confederate battle flag. Breyer, J., for the Court (5 to 4) held Texas's specialty license plate designs constitute government speech, and thus Texas was entitled to refuse to issue plates. Texas did not violate the nonprofit organization's free speech rights by denying its application for a design that included the Confederate flag. Texas "need not issue plates praising Florida's oranges as far better." Texas offers plates that say, "Fight Terrorism," but "it need not issue plates promoting al Qaeda." Drivers who display a State's selected license plate designs convey the messages communicated through those designs. The state could not compel a private party to express a view with which the private party disagrees, *Wooley v. Maynard*, 430 U.S. 705, 97 S.Ct. 1428, 51 L.Ed.2d 752 (1977)(state cannot require motor vehicles to bear license plates embossed with the state motto, "Live Free or Die"). Similarly, the Sons of Confederate Veterans cannot force Texas to include a Confederate battle flag on its specialty license plates. "Texas license plates are, essentially, government IDs. And issuers of ID 'typically do not permit' the placement on their IDs of 'message[s] with which they do not wish to be associated,' " quoting *Summum*.

Alito, J., dissented, joined by Roberts, C.J., Scalia & Kennedy, JJ. "Here is a test. Suppose you sat by the side of a Texas highway and studied the license plates on the vehicles passing by. You would see, in addition to the standard Texas plates, an impressive array of specialty plates. (There are now more than 350 varieties.) You would likely observe plates that honor numerous colleges and universities. You might see plates bearing the name of a high school, a fraternity, or sorority, the Masons, the Knights of Columbus, the Daughters of the American Revolution, a realty company, a favorite soft drink, a favorite burger restaurant, and a favorite NASCAR driver." He then asked, "would you really think that the sentiments reflected in these specialty plates are the views of the State of Texas and not those of the owners of the cars?" How would you respond to that argument?

Matal v. Tam, 582 U.S. ___, 137 S.Ct. 1744, ___ L.Ed.2d ___, 2017 WL 2621315 (2017). A trademark applicant objected when the Patent and Trademark Office refused to register its trademark "THE SLANTS" (an Asian rock band) because that mark disparaged people of Asian descent. Alito, J., for the Court, held that disparagement clause of the Lanham Act, prohibiting federal trademark registration for marks that might disparage any persons, living or dead, was facially invalid under the First Amendment.[1] The "PTO has denied registration to 'Abort the Republicans' (disparaging to Republicans), 'Democrats Shouldn't Breed' (disparaging to Democrats), and a logo consisting of the communist hammer-and-sickle with a slash through it (disparaging to Soviets)."[2]

Matal held that trademarks are not government speech: "The Federal Government does not dream up these marks, and it does not edit marks submitted for registration." Moreover, the "government speech" doctrine is "susceptible to dangerous misuse." "If private speech could be passed off as government speech by simply affixing a government seal of approval, government could silence or muffle the expression of disfavored viewpoints."

A separate opinion of Alito, J., joined by Roberts, C.J., and Thomas, & Breyer, JJ., also rejected the government's argument that trademarks are subsidized speech because this case does not involve cash subsidies. They added it was unnecessary to decide if trademarks are Commercial Speech because the disparagement clause cannot survive the lessened scrutiny the Court applies in Commercial Speech cases. They added:

> An amicus supporting the Government refers to "encouraging racial tolerance and protecting the privacy and welfare of individuals." Brief for Native American Organizations as Amici Curiae 21. But no matter how the point is phrased, its unmistakable thrust is this: The Government has an interest in preventing speech expressing ideas that offend. And, as we have explained, that idea strikes at the heart of the First Amendment. Speech that demeans on the basis of race, ethnicity, gender, religion, age, disability, or any other similar ground is hateful; but the proudest boast of our free speech jurisprudence is that we protect the freedom to express "the thought that we hate."

Kennedy's separate opinion agreed that the disparagement clause constitutes viewpoint discrimination because it reflects the government's disapproval of certain speech, and that heightened scrutiny should apply, whether or not trademarks are commercial speech.

---

1 In addition, Alito, J., joined by Roberts, C.J., Thomas & Breyer, JJ., wrote a concurring opinion. Kennedy, J. concurred in part and concurred in the judgment, joined by Ginsburg, Sotomayor, & Kagan, JJ. Thomas, J., filed an opinion concurring in part and concurring in the judgment. Justice Gorsuch took no part in the consideration or decision of the case.

2 Amicus Brief of Brief of the Cato Institute and a Basket of Deplorable People and Organizations as Amici Curiae Supporting Respondent, in *Lee v. Tam,* 2016 WL 7405919 (December 16, 2016, U.S.)

10–4 FIGHTING WORDS AND HOSTILE AUDIENCES

Unabridged, p. 1107; add at end of case, add new *Note*:

Abridged, p. 863; add to end of *Notes*, new Note 3:

Elonis v. United States, 576 U.S.___, 135 S.Ct. 2001, 192 L. Ed. 2d 1 (2015). Elonis posted rap lyrics on his Facebook page containing graphically violent language and imagery about his ex-wife, coworkers, a kindergarten class, and state and federal law enforcement. His posts included disclaimers stating that the lyrics were fictitious and that he was exercising his First Amendment rights. Many people who knew him viewed his posts as threatening. His boss fired him for threatening co-workers, and his wife obtained a state court protection-from-abuse order against him. The FBI monitored him and eventually arrested him. The jury convicted him of violating 18 U.S.C. § 875(c), which makes it a crime to transmit in interstate commerce "any communication containing any threat" to "injure the person of another." The jury instruction was that Elonis was guilty if a *reasonable person* would interpret his statements as a threat. That instruction did not require the jury to determine the defendant's "mental state."

Chief Justice Roberts, for the Court, reversed and held that courts should generally interpret criminal statutes to include a *scienter* requirement and *mens rea* even when the statute does not contain them. Did the speaker act with a *subjective* intent to threaten? A " 'reasonable person' standard is a familiar feature of civil liability in tort law, but is inconsistent with 'the conventional requirement for criminal conduct—*awareness* of some wrongdoing.' " (Emphasis in original). Given the statutory interpretation, "it is not necessary to consider any First Amendment issues."

10–9 THE RIGHT OF ASSOCIATION

10–9.3 PATRONAGE DISMISSALS

Unabridged, p. 1196; add to end of *Notes*, new Note 7:

7. *Heffernan v. City of Patterson*, 578 U.S. ___, 136 S.Ct. 1412, 194 L.Ed.2d 508 (2016). Jeffrey Heffernan, a police officer in Patterson, New Jersey, picked up, at the request of his bedridden mother, a campaign sign of the candidate running against the sitting Patterson mayor. The candidate was also a friend of Heffernan's. Other members of the Patterson police force saw him, sign in hand, talking to campaign workers, and so the chief of police and Heffernan's supervisor (both of whom the incumbent mayor had appointed) learned about it. The next day, Heffernan's supervisors demoted him from detective to patrol officer. He sued the City, claiming that the police chief and supervisor had deprived him of a "right . . . secured by the Constitution" in violation of 42 U.S.C. § 1983. The district court and Third Circuit Court of Appeals ruled against Heffernan, concluding that although the defendants

demoted him because they thought he was engaging in political activity (which is constitutionally protected), he was not, in fact, engaged in a constitutionally protected activity. The Court (6 to 2) reversed. Breyer, J., for the Court held that motive of the employer, not the employee, is key because the First Amendment prevents the employer from retaliating against Heffernan based on its mistaken belief that he had engaged in protected speech. This rule tracks the language of the First Amendment, which focuses on the Government's activity. Moreover, the constitutional harm (discouraging employees from engaging in protected speech) is the same, whether or not the employer's action rests on a factual mistake.

The employee still bears the burden of proving an improper employer motive. It is possible that the employer demoted Heffernan because of a neutral policy prohibiting him from overt involvement in any political campaign. The Court remanded for the lower courts to decide if that policy existed, whether Heffernan's supervisors followed it, and whether that standard is constitutional.

Thomas, J., joined by Alito J., dissented and argued that the City, although it demoted Heffernan to retaliate against his political beliefs, did not violate free speech because Heffernan did not intend to engage in First Amendment activity.

10–11 CAMPAIGN SPEECH AND FINANCING

Unabridged, p. 1264; add to Note 5, after *Republican Party of Minnesota v. White*:

Abridged, p. 974; add to Note 4, after *Republican Party of Minnesota v. White*:

The Florida Supreme Court adopted Canon 7C(1) of its Code of Judicial Conduct (corresponding to ABA Model Judicial Code, Rule 4.1(A)(8), which provides that judicial candidates "shall not personally solicit campaign funds . . . but may establish committees of responsible persons" to raise money for election campaigns. Chief Justice Roberts, for a fractured Court (5 to 4), held that that Florida has a compelling interest in "preserving the public confidence in the integrity of its judiciary" and that this prohibition on personal solicitation is narrowly tailored to avoid unnecessarily abridging speech. *Williams-Yulee v. Florida Bar*, 575 U.S. ___, 135 S.Ct. 1656, 191 L. Ed. 2d 570 (2015). This is "one of the rare cases in which a speech restriction withstands strict scrutiny." The Florida (and the ABA) Rule require judges and judicial candidates to direct campaign committees to solicit contributions. While personal solicitation and committee solicitation might operate the same in substance, "a State may conclude that they present markedly different appearances to the public."

Williams-Yulee drafted a letter announcing her candidacy for judicial office and in that letter asked for contributions to her political campaign. She also posted the letter online. She lost the primary and the Florida Bar filed a complaint against her for violating the solicitation rule. The Florida Supreme Court upheld a public reprimand of Ms. Williams-Yulee. The Rule provides that the judicial candidate "shall not personally solicit campaign funds." Williams-Yulee accepted that the State could forbid face-to-face solicitation, but she never engaged in any face-to-face solicitation. She never walked up to a contributor who handed her a $100 bill. Instead, she wrote a letter, signed it, mailed it to local voters, and posted it on her website. Her actions violated this Rule, which required her to set up a committee to solicit the funds.

Scalia, J., filed a dissenting opinion, which Thomas, J., joined. Kennedy & Alito, J.J., also filed dissenting opinions. The Florida Rule specifically permits judicial candidates to write thank you notes to campaign donors, so candidates know who contributed and who did not. This Rule also did not ban judicial candidates from personally asking individuals for personal gifts or loans as long as the gift or loan is not a campaign contribution—that is, the donor did not give it for the purpose of influencing the results of an election. Williams-Yulee may not write a letter asking for campaign contribution from her parents who has no chance of appearing in her court. Yet, the Rule allows her personally to solicit donations to help her fight the Florida Bar's charges.

CHAPTER 11

RELIGION

■ ■ ■

11–3 RELIGIOUSLY BASED EXCEPTIONS TO STATE IMPOSED DUTIES

Unabridged, p. 1447; add to Note 3, after *Cutter v. Wilkinson*:

Abridged, p. 1109; add to end of Note 2:

Holt v. Hobbs, 574 U.S. ___, 135 S.Ct. 853, 190 L.Ed.2d 747 (2015). A Muslim prisoner wanted to grow a ½-inch beard in accordance with his religious beliefs. He sued the Director of Arkansas Department of Correction, challenging under the Religious Land Use and Institutionalized Persons Act (RLUIPA) the denial of a religious accommodation under Department's grooming policy. Alito, J., for the Court, held that this grooming policy substantially burdened the prisoner's exercise of religion. The Department does have a compelling interest in preventing prisoners from hiding contraband, or disguising their identities, but this beard policy is not the least restrictive means of implementing that interest. The prison could not show why the security risk presented by a prisoner shaving a ½-inch beard is so different from the risk of a prisoner shaving a mustache, head hair, or ¼-inch beard. Similarly, the prison did not explain why the risk that a prisoner will shave a ½-inch beard to disguise himself is so great that the prison cannot allow ½-inch beards even though it allows prisoners to grow mustaches, head hair, or ¼-inch beards for medical/ dermatological reasons.

The district court was also erred in suggesting that the burden on the prisoner's religious exercise was slight because he testified that his religion would "credit" him for attempting to follow his religious beliefs, even if that attempt proved to be unsuccessful. "RLUIPA, however, applies to an exercise of religion regardless of whether it is 'compelled.' "

Unabridged, p. 1450; add to end of Note 4:

Abridged, p. 1110; add to end of Note 3:

Zubik v. Burwell, 578 U.S. ___, 136 S.Ct. 1557, 194 L.Ed.2d. 269 (2016)(per curiam). Various nonprofit religious groups, led by the Little Sisters of the Poor (an order of Catholic nuns who run hospices), objected that the Secretary of Health and Human Services required them to offer an insurance plan including abortion-causing drugs. They had no problem with the federal government providing such services or the Government paying for them. They just did not want to be complicit.

During the oral argument, Justice Alito asked the Solicitor General whether it was a substantial burden for a female employee of a religious organization to go on her state exchange to purchase a separate contraceptive policy (which the federal government could pay for if it wanted to do so). The Solicitor General responded that it was a "hassle" to use the state or federal exchange, but Chief Justice Roberts (perhaps smiling) said, "I've heard about how easy it is [to use the health exchanges]." The Government argued that its mandate was necessary for employees to have "seamless coverage, but Petitioners argued that the Government tolerated or created non-seamless coverage for millions of other employees.[1]

The petitioners' briefs pointed out that "tens of millions of people" are in grandfathered plans not subject to the mandate, and there is no requirement that these plans "ever be phased out." The Government's purpose for exempting millions from this contraception/abortifacients mandate is merely to "promote administrative convenience."[2] The Government also exempts millions of other employees from this contraceptive/abortifacients coverage because they work for small employers, or, Petitioners argued, the Government created arcane or irrational distinctions.[3] Petitioners argued that this Government mandate is not a neutral law of general applicability that governed religious and nonreligious alike.

After oral argument, the Court took the unusual step of asking the litigants to submit supplemental briefs on whether there could be an "accommodation" to avoid compromising religious convictions. The religious groups proposed that the federal government require insurance companies to create stand-alone contraception plans for workers at religiously affiliated institutions "with separate enrollment processes, insurance cards, payment sources, and communication streams." The petitioners' brief explained, "Under a truly independent scheme, such employers wouldn't be complying with that mandate at all. They would be exempt from that mandate, and the commercial insurer would be complying with a separate mandate imposed by the federal government." The Government "confirmed that the challenged procedures 'for

---

[1] Petitioners argued, because "the Government has decided not to mandate contraceptive coverage at all in connection with grandfathered plans and [certain] 'religious employer' plans, it cannot claim a compelling interest in mandating 'seamless' coverage in connection with Petitioners' plans." Brief of Petitioners, *Zubik v. Burwell*, 2016 WL 93988 *70 (U.S. 2016).

[2] The Government estimated that 37% of private employers in the country offer at least one grandfathered health plan, and 26% of employees nationwide are enrolled in a grandfathered plan. "In total, at least 33.9 million people are on private-sector grandfathered plans, and 10.7 million people are on state- and local-government grandfathered plans. See 80 Fed. Reg. 72,192, 72,218 (Nov. 18, 2015)." Brief of Petitioners, *Zubik v. Burwell*, 2016 WL 93988 * 7 (U.S. 2016).

[3] For example, the Government did not exempt the Catholic Charities of Pittsburgh because it is incorporated separately from the Diocese of Pittsburgh. Its counterpart, Catholic Charities of Erie, is as a department of the Roman Catholic Diocese of Erie. Because of this formal difference, the Government ordered Catholic Charities of Pittsburgh to comply with the mandate, but not the Catholic Charities of Erie, considered part of an "exempt" religious employer. Brief of Petitioners, *Zubik v. Burwell*, 2016 WL 93988 *58 (U.S. 2016).

employers with insured plans could be modified to operate in the manner posited in the Court's order while still ensuring that the affected women receive contraceptive coverage seamlessly, together with the rest of their health coverage.' " Consequently, the Court remanded to give the parties the opportunity to "arrive at an approach going forward that accommodates petitioners' religious exercise while at the same time ensuring that women covered by petitioners' health plans "receive full and equal health coverage, including contraceptive coverage."

In the meantime, "the Government may not impose taxes or penalties on petitioners for failure to provide the relevant notice." The Court added that it expressed no view on the merits of the case. Sotomayor, J., concurred, joined by Ginsburg, J., noting that the lower courts should not construe today's opinion as an expression of the Court's views on the merits.

Unabridged, p. 1450; add new case after the *Notes*:

Abridged, p. 1110; add new case after the *Notes*:

TRINITY LUTHERAN CHURCH OF COLUMBIA, INC. V. COMER

137 S.Ct. 2012, ___ L.Ed.2d ___, ___ 2017 WL 2722410 (2017).

CHIEF JUSTICE ROBERTS delivered the opinion of the Court, except as to footnote 3.

The Missouri Department of Natural Resources offers state grants to help public and private schools, nonprofit daycare centers, and other nonprofit entities purchase rubber playground surfaces made from recycled tires. Trinity Lutheran Church applied for such a grant for its preschool and daycare center and would have received one, but for the fact that Trinity Lutheran is a church. The Department had a policy of categorically disqualifying churches and other religious organizations from receiving grants under its playground resurfacing program. The question presented is whether the Department's policy violated the rights of Trinity Lutheran under the Free Exercise Clause of the First Amendment.

The Trinity Lutheran Church Child Learning Center is a preschool and daycare center open throughout the year to serve working families in Boone County, Missouri, and the surrounding area. [T]he Center merged with Trinity Lutheran Church in 1985 and operates under its auspices on church property. The Center admits students of any religion, and enrollment stands at about 90 children ranging from age two to five.

The Center includes a playground that is equipped with the basic playground essentials: slides, swings, jungle gyms, monkey bars, and sandboxes. Almost the entire surface beneath and surrounding the play equipment is coarse pea gravel. Youngsters, of course, often fall on the playground or tumble from the equipment. And when they do, the gravel can be unforgiving.

In 2012, the Center sought to replace a large portion of the pea gravel with a pour-in-place rubber surface by participating in Missouri's Scrap Tire Program. Run by the State's Department of Natural Resources to reduce the number of used tires destined for landfills and dump sites, the program offers reimbursement grants to qualifying nonprofit organizations that purchase playground surfaces made from recycled tires. It is funded through a fee imposed on the sale of new tires in the State.

Due to limited resources, the Department cannot offer grants to all applicants and so awards them on a competitive basis to those scoring highest based on several criteria, such as the poverty level of the population in the surrounding area and the applicant's plan to promote recycling. When the Center applied, the Department had a strict and express policy of denying grants to any applicant owned or controlled by a church, sect, or other religious entity. That policy, in the Department's view, was compelled by Article I, Section 7 of the Missouri Constitution, which provides:

> "That no money shall ever be taken from the public treasury, directly or indirectly, in aid of any church, sect or denomination of religion, or in aid of any priest, preacher, minister or teacher thereof, as such; and that no preference shall be given to nor any discrimination made against any church, sect or creed of religion, or any form of religious faith or worship."

In its application, the Center disclosed its status as a ministry of Trinity Lutheran Church and specified that the Center's mission was "to provide a safe, clean, and attractive school facility in conjunction with an educational program structured to allow a child to grow spiritually, physically, socially, and cognitively." App. to Pet. for Cert. 131a. . . .

The Center ranked fifth among the 44 applicants in the 2012 Scrap Tire Program. But despite its high score, the Center was deemed categorically ineligible to receive a grant. [T]he program director explained that, under Article I, Section 7 of the Missouri Constitution, the Department could not provide financial assistance directly to a church. The Department ultimately awarded 14 grants as part of the 2012 program. Because the Center was operated by Trinity Lutheran Church, it did not receive a grant.

Trinity Lutheran sued the Director of the Department in Federal District Court. The Church alleged that the Department's failure to approve the Center's application, pursuant to its policy of denying grants to religiously affiliated applicants, violates the Free Exercise Clause of the First Amendment. Trinity Lutheran sought declaratory and injunctive relief prohibiting the Department from discriminating against the Church on that basis in future grant applications.

The District Court granted the Department's motion to dismiss [and] the Eighth Circuit affirmed. The court recognized that it was "rather clear" that Missouri *could* award a scrap tire grant to Trinity Lutheran without running afoul of the Establishment Clause of the United States Constitution. But, the Court of Appeals explained, that did not mean the Free Exercise Clause compelled the State to disregard the antiestablishment principle reflected in its own Constitution. . . . We granted certiorari and now reverse.

The First Amendment provides, in part, that "Congress shall make no law respecting an establishment of religion, or prohibiting the free exercise thereof." The parties agree that the Establishment Clause of that Amendment does not prevent Missouri from including Trinity Lutheran in the Scrap Tire Program. That does not, however, answer the question under the Free Exercise Clause, because we have recognized that there is "play in the joints" between what the Establishment Clause permits and the Free Exercise Clause compels. *Locke* [*v. Davey*] (internal quotation marks omitted).*

The Free Exercise Clause "protect[s] religious observers against unequal treatment" and subjects to the strictest scrutiny laws that target the religious for "special disabilities" based on their "religious status." *Church of Lukumi Babalu Aye, Inc. v. Hialeah*, 508 U.S. 520, 533, 542 (1993) (internal quotation marks omitted). Applying that basic principle, this Court has repeatedly confirmed that denying a generally available benefit solely on account of religious identity imposes a penalty on the free exercise of religion that can be justified only by a state interest 'of the highest order.' *McDaniel v. Paty*, 435 U.S. 618, 628 (1978) (plurality opinion) (quoting *Wisconsin v. Yoder*, 406 U.S. 205, 215 (1972)).

In *Everson v. Board of Education of Ewing*, 330 U.S. 1 (1947), for example, we upheld against an Establishment Clause challenge a New Jersey law enabling a local school *district* to reimburse parents for the public transportation costs of sending their children to public and private schools, including parochial schools. In the course of ruling that the Establishment Clause allowed New Jersey to extend that public benefit to all its citizens regardless of their religious belief, we explained that a State 'cannot hamper its citizens in the free exercise of their own religion. Consequently, it cannot exclude individual Catholics, Lutherans, Mohammedans, Baptists, Jews, Methodists, Non-believers, Presbyterians, or the members of any other faith, *because of their faith, or lack of it*, from receiving the benefits of public welfare legislation.' *Id.*, at 16.

Three decades later, in *McDaniel v. Paty*, the Court struck down under the Free Exercise Clause a Tennessee statute disqualifying ministers from serving as delegates to the State's constitutional convention. Writing for

* [Editor's Note: *Locke v. Davey*, 540 U.S. 712, 124 S.Ct. 1307, 158 L. Ed. 2d 1 (2004), held that a state did not violate Free Exercise Clause by refusing to fund devotional theology instruction.]

the plurality, Chief Justice Burger acknowledged that Tennessee had disqualified ministers from serving as legislators since the adoption of its first Constitution in 1796, and that a number of early States had also disqualified ministers from legislative office. This historical tradition, however, did not change the fact that the statute discriminated against McDaniel by denying him a benefit solely because of his "*status* as a 'minister.' " McDaniel could not seek to participate in the convention while also maintaining his role as a minister; to pursue the one, he would have to give up the other. In this way, said Chief Justice Burger, the Tennessee law "effectively penalizes the free exercise of [McDaniel's] constitutional liberties," quoting *Sherbert v. Verner*, (1963); internal quotation marks omitted). Joined by Justice Marshall in concurrence, Justice Brennan added that "because the challenged provision requires [McDaniel] to purchase his right to engage in the ministry by sacrificing his candidacy it impairs the free exercise of his religion." *McDaniel*, 435 U.S., at 634.

In recent years, when this Court has rejected free exercise challenges, the laws in question have been neutral and generally applicable without regard to religion. We have been careful to distinguish such laws from those that single out the religious for disfavored treatment.

For example, in *Lyng v. Northwest Indian Cemetery Protective Association*, 485 U.S. 439 (1988), we held that the Free Exercise Clause did not prohibit the Government from timber harvesting or road construction on a particular tract of federal land, even though the Government's action would obstruct the religious practice of several Native American Tribes that held certain sites on the tract to be sacred. . . . The Court specifically noted, however, that the Government action did not "penalize religious activity by denying any person an equal share of the rights, benefits, and privileges enjoyed by other citizens."

[I]n *Church of Lukumi Babalu Aye, Inc. v. Hialeah*, we struck down three facially neutral city ordinances that outlawed certain forms of animal slaughter. Members of the Santeria religion challenged the ordinances under the Free Exercise Clause, alleging that despite their facial neutrality, the ordinances had a discriminatory purpose easy to ferret out: prohibiting sacrificial rituals integral to Santeria but distasteful to local residents. We agreed. [C]iting *McDaniel* and *Smith*, we restated the now-familiar refrain: The Free Exercise Clause protects against laws that " 'impose[ ] special disabilities on the basis of . . . religious status.' "

The Department's policy expressly discriminates against otherwise eligible recipients by disqualifying them from a public benefit solely because of their religious character. If the cases just described make one thing clear, it is that such a policy imposes a penalty on the free exercise of religion that triggers the most exacting scrutiny. This conclusion is unremarkable in light of our prior decisions.

Like the disqualification statute in *McDaniel*, the Department's policy puts Trinity Lutheran to a choice: It may participate in an otherwise available benefit program or remain a religious institution. Of course, Trinity Lutheran is free to continue operating as a church, just as McDaniel was free to continue being a minister. But that freedom comes at the cost of automatic and absolute exclusion from the benefits of a public program for which the Center is otherwise fully qualified. And when the State conditions a benefit in this way, *McDaniel* says plainly that the State has punished the free exercise of religion: "To condition the availability of benefits . . . upon [a recipient's] willingness to . . . surrender[ ] his religiously impelled [status] effectively penalizes the free exercise of his constitutional liberties." (plurality opinion) (alterations omitted).

The Department contends that merely declining to extend funds to Trinity Lutheran does not *prohibit* the Church from engaging in any religious conduct or otherwise exercising its religious rights. In this sense, says the Department, its policy is unlike the ordinances struck down in *Lukumi*, which outlawed rituals central to Santeria. Here the Department has simply declined to allocate to Trinity Lutheran a subsidy the State had no obligation to provide in the first place. That decision does not meaningfully burden the Church's free exercise rights. And absent any such burden, the argument continues, the Department is free to heed the State's antiestablishment objection to providing funds directly to a church.

It is true the Department has not criminalized the way Trinity Lutheran worships or told the Church that it cannot subscribe to a certain view of the Gospel. But, as the Department itself acknowledges, the Free Exercise Clause protects against "indirect coercion or penalties on the free exercise of religion, not just outright prohibitions." *Lyng*. As the Court put it more than 50 years ago, "[i]t is too late in the day to doubt that the liberties of religion and expression may be infringed by the denial of or placing of conditions upon a benefit or privilege." *Sherbert*; see also *McDaniel*, 435 U.S., at 633 (Brennan, J., concurring in judgment) (The 'proposition—that the law does not interfere with free exercise because it does not directly prohibit religious activity, but merely conditions eligibility for office on its abandonment—is . . . squarely rejected by precedent').

Trinity Lutheran is not claiming any entitlement to a subsidy. It instead asserts a right to participate in a government benefit program without having to disavow its religious character. The "imposition of such a condition upon even a gratuitous benefit inevitably deter[s] or discourage[s] the exercise of First Amendment rights." The express discrimination against religious exercise here is not the denial of a grant, but rather the refusal to allow the Church—solely because it is a church—to compete with secular organizations for a grant.

The Department attempts to get out from under the weight of our precedents by arguing that the free exercise question in this case is instead controlled by our decision in *Locke v. Davey*. It is not. In *Locke*, the State of Washington created a scholarship program to assist high-achieving students with the costs of postsecondary education. The scholarships were paid out of the State's general fund, and eligibility was based on criteria such as an applicant's score on college admission tests and family income. While scholarship recipients were free to use the money at accredited religious and non-religious schools alike, they were not permitted to use the funds to pursue a devotional theology degree—one "devotional in nature or designed to induce religious faith." (internal quotation marks omitted). Davey was selected for a scholarship but was denied the funds when he refused to certify that he would not use them toward a devotional degree. He sued, arguing that the State's refusal to allow its scholarship money to go toward such degrees violated his free exercise rights.

This Court disagreed. [T]he State had "merely chosen not to fund a distinct category of instruction." Davey was not denied a scholarship because of who he *was*; he was denied a scholarship because of what he proposed *to do*—use the funds to prepare for the ministry. Here there is no question that Trinity Lutheran was denied a grant simply because of what it is—a church.

The Court in *Locke* also stated that Washington's choice was in keeping with the State's antiestablishment interest in not using taxpayer funds to pay for the training of clergy; in fact, the Court could "think of few areas in which a State's antiestablishment interests come more into play." The claimant in *Locke* sought funding for an "essentially religious endeavor . . . akin to a religious calling as well as an academic pursuit," and opposition to such funding "to support church leaders" lay at the historic core of the Religion Clauses. Here nothing of the sort can be said about a program to use recycled tires to resurface playgrounds.

. . . *Locke* took account of Washington's antiestablishment interest only after determining, as noted, that the scholarship program did not "require students to choose between their religious beliefs and receiving a government benefit." 540 U.S., at 720–721 (citing *McDaniel*, 435 U.S. 618). As the Court put it, Washington's scholarship program went "a long way toward including religion in its benefits." Students in the program were free to use their scholarships at "pervasively religious schools." Davey could use his scholarship to pursue a secular degree at one institution while studying devotional theology at another. He could also use his scholarship money to attend a religious college and take devotional theology courses there. The only thing he could not do was use the scholarship to pursue a degree in that subject.

In this case, there is no dispute that Trinity Lutheran *is* put to the choice between being a church and receiving a government benefit. The rule is simple: No churches need apply.[3]

The State in this case expressly requires Trinity Lutheran to renounce its religious character in order to participate in an otherwise generally available public benefit program, for which it is fully qualified. Our cases make clear that such a condition imposes a penalty on the free exercise of religion that must be subjected to the "most rigorous" scrutiny. *Lukumi*.[4] . . .

The State has pursued its preferred policy to the point of expressly denying a qualified religious entity a public benefit solely because of its religious character. Under our precedents, that goes too far. The Department's policy violates the Free Exercise Clause. . . .

JUSTICE GORSUCH, with whom JUSTICE THOMAS joins, concurring in part.

Missouri's law bars Trinity Lutheran from participating in a public benefits program only because it is a church. I agree this violates the First Amendment and I am pleased to join nearly all of the Court's opinion. I offer only two modest qualifications.

First, the Court leaves open the possibility a useful distinction might be drawn between laws that discriminate on the basis of religious *status* and religious *use*. Respectfully, I harbor doubts about the stability of such a line. Does a religious man say grace before dinner? Or does a man begin his meal in a religious manner? Is it a religious group that built the playground? Or did a group build the playground so it might be used to advance a religious mission? . . .

Neither do I see why the First Amendment's Free Exercise Clause should care. After all, that Clause guarantees the free *exercise* of religion, not just the right to inward belief (or status). And this Court has long explained that government may not "devise mechanisms, overt or disguised, designed to persecute or oppress a religion or its practices." Generally, the government may not force people to choose between participation in a public program and their right to free exercise of religion. I don't see why it should matter whether we describe that benefit, say, as closed to Lutherans (status) or closed to people who do Lutheran things (use). It is free exercise either way.

---

[3] This case involves express discrimination based on religious identity with respect to playground resurfacing. We do not address religious uses of funding or other forms of discrimination.

[4] We have held that "a law targeting religious beliefs as such is never permissible." *Lukumi*; see also *McDaniel v. Paty* (1978) (plurality opinion). We do not need to decide whether the condition Missouri imposes in this case falls within the scope of that rule, because it cannot survive strict scrutiny in any event.

For these reasons, reliance on the status-use distinction does not suffice for me to distinguish *Locke v. Davey*, 540 U.S. 712 (2004). In that case, this Court upheld a funding restriction barring a student from using a scholarship to pursue a degree in devotional theology. But can it really matter whether the restriction in *Locke* was phrased in terms of use instead of status (for was it a student who wanted a vocational degree in religion? or was it a religious student who wanted the necessary education for his chosen vocation?). If that case can be correct and distinguished, it seems it might be only because of the opinion's claim of a long tradition against the use of public funds for training of the clergy, a tradition the Court correctly explains has no analogue here.

Second and for similar reasons, I am unable to join the footnoted observation, n. 3, that "[t]his case involves express discrimination based on religious identity with respect to playground resurfacing." Of course the footnote is entirely correct, but I worry that some might mistakenly read it to suggest that only "playground resurfacing" cases, or only those with some association with children's safety or health, or perhaps some other social good we find sufficiently worthy, are governed by the legal rules recounted in and faithfully applied by the Court's opinion. Such a reading would be unreasonable for our cases are "governed by general principles, rather than ad hoc improvisations." And the general principles here do not permit discrimination against religious exercise—whether on the playground or anywhere else.

JUSTICE BREYER, concurring in the judgment. . . .

The Court stated in *Everson* that "cutting off church schools from" such "general government services as ordinary police and fire protection . . . is obviously not the purpose of the First Amendment." Here, the State would cut Trinity Lutheran off from participation in a general program designed to secure or to improve the health and safety of children. I see no significant difference. The fact that the program at issue ultimately funds only a limited number of projects cannot itself justify a religious distinction. Nor is there any administrative or other reason to treat church schools differently. The sole reason advanced that explains the difference is faith. And it is that last-mentioned fact that calls the Free Exercise Clause into play. We need not go further. Public benefits come in many shapes and sizes. I would leave the application of the Free Exercise Clause to other kinds of public benefits for another day.

JUSTICE SOTOMAYOR, with whom JUSTICE GINSBURG joins, dissenting.

To hear the Court tell it, this is a simple case about recycling tires to resurface a playground. The stakes are higher. This case is about nothing less than the relationship between religious institutions and the civil government—that is, between church and state. The Court today profoundly changes that relationship by holding, for the first time, that the

Constitution requires the government to provide public funds directly to a church. Its decision slights both our precedents and our history, and its reasoning weakens this country's longstanding commitment to a separation of church and state beneficial to both.

Founded in 1922, Trinity Lutheran Church (Church) "operates . . . for the express purpose of carrying out the commission of . . . Jesus Christ as directed to His church on earth" Our Story, http://www.trinity-lcms.org/story (all internet materials as last visited June 22, 2017). The Church uses "preaching, teaching, worship, witness, service, and fellowship according to the Word of God" to carry out its mission "to 'make disciples.'" Mission, http://www.trinity-lcms.org/mission (quoting Matthew 28:18–20). The Church's religious beliefs include its desire to "associat[e] with the [Trinity Church Child] Learning Center." App. to Pet. for Cert. Located on Church property, the Learning Center provides daycare and preschool for about "90 children ages two to kindergarten." *Id.*

The Learning Center serves as "a ministry of the Church and incorporates daily religion and developmentally appropriate activities into . . . [its] program." *Id.* In this way, "[t]hrough the Learning Center, the Church teaches a Christian world view to children of members of the Church, as well as children of non-member residents" of the area. These activities represent the Church's "sincere religious belief . . . to use [the Learning Center] to teach the Gospel to children of its members, as well to bring the Gospel message to non-members."

[I]t is surprising that the Court mentions the Establishment Clause only to note the parties' agreement that it "does not prevent Missouri from including Trinity Lutheran in the Scrap Tire Program." Constitutional questions are decided by this Court, not the parties' concessions. The Establishment Clause does not allow Missouri to grant the Church's funding request because the Church uses the Learning Center, including its playground, in conjunction with its religious mission. The Court's silence on this front signals either its misunderstanding of the facts of this case or a startling departure from our precedents.

. . . The Church seeks state funds to improve the Learning Center's facilities, which, by the Church's own avowed description, are used to assist the spiritual growth of the children of its members and to spread the Church's faith to the children of nonmembers. The Church's playground surface—like a Sunday School room's walls or the sanctuary's pews—are integrated with and integral to its religious mission. The conclusion that the funding the Church seeks would impermissibly advance religion is inescapable.

[A] prophylactic rule against the use of public funds for houses of worship is a permissible accommodation of these weighty interests. . . . Today, thirty-eight States have a counterpart to Missouri's Article I, § 7.

The provisions, as a general matter, date back to or before these States' original Constitutions. That so many States have for so long drawn a line that prohibits public funding for houses of worship, based on principles rooted in this Nation's understanding of how best to foster religious liberty, supports the conclusion that public funding of houses of worship "is of a different ilk."

. . . The Scrap Tire Program offers not a generally available benefit but a selective benefit for a few recipients each year. In this context, the comparison to truly generally available benefits is inapt.

On top of all of this, the Court's application of its new rule here is mistaken. . . . The constitutional provisions of thirty-nine States—all but invalidated today—the weighty interests they protect, and the history they draw on deserve more than this judicial brush aside. . . .

Today's decision discounts centuries of history and jeopardizes the government's ability to remain secular. . . .

The Court today dismantles a core protection for religious freedom provided in these Clauses. It holds not just that a government may support houses of worship with taxpayer funds, but that—at least in this case and perhaps in others,—it must do so whenever it decides to create a funding program. History shows that the Religion Clauses separate the public treasury from religious coffers as one measure to secure the kind of freedom of conscience that benefits both religion and government. If this separation means anything, it means that the government cannot, or at the very least need not, tax its citizens and turn that money over to houses of worship. The Court today blinds itself to the outcome this history requires and leads us instead to a place where separation of church and state is a constitutional slogan, not a constitutional commitment. I dissent.

[The Opinion of THOMAS, J., joined by GORSUCH, J., concurring in part, is omitted.]

NOTES

1. The dissent notes that Missouri's Constitutional provision in this case, is found in thirty-nine States, and they are "all but invalidated today." These amendments are often called Blaine Amendments, which historians say were rooted in 19th century anti-Catholic bigotry. They were designed to prevent any state aid that might go to Catholic parochial schools.* Republican

* See, *e.g.,* U.S. Commission on Civil Rights, *School Choice: The Blaine Amendments & Anti-Catholicism* (2007), http://www.usccr.gov/pubs/BlaineReport.pdf; PHILIP HAMBURGER, SEPARATION OF CHURCH AND STATE 335 (Harvard Univ. Press, 2002) (Nativist Protestants "failed to obtain a federal constitutional amendment but, because of the strength of anti-Catholic feeling, managed to secure local versions of the Blaine amendment in the vast majority of the states.") Douglas Laycock, *The Underlying Unity of Separation and Neutrality*, 46 Emory L.J. 43, 50 (1997)("Although there were legitimate arguments made on both sides, the nineteenth century

Congressman (and then Senator) James G. Blaine from Maine proposed a federal constitutional amendment to forbid any use of public funds to support religious schools, which were typically Catholic. That proposed U.S. Constitutional Amendment did not pass Congress, but many states enacted their versions of the Blaine Amendment and some states have used them to deny school aid or vouchers to religiously affiliated schools.

Note that in footnote 4 the Court says, "We have held that 'a law targeting religious beliefs as such is never permissible.' We do not need to decide whether the condition Missouri imposes in this case falls within the scope of that rule, because it cannot survive strict scrutiny in any event." (Internal citations omitted). Hence, the Court did not examine whether the state versions of the Blaine Amendment intended to target a particular religion.

2. The day after the Court decided *Trinity Lutheran*, it vacated and remanded two cases in light of *Trinity Lutheran* (1) a New Mexico Supreme Court decision that prevented students at religious schools from receiving state-funded textbooks. *New Mexico Ass'n of Non-public Schools v. Moses*, ___ S.Ct. ___, 2017 WL 2742852 (2017), and (2), a Colorado Supreme Court ruling that prohibited a school choice program, because students at religious schools were allowed to participate. *Colorado State Board of Education v. Taxpayers for Public Education*, ___ S.Ct. ___, 2017 WL 2742851 (2017).

---

opposition to funding religious schools drew heavily on anti-Catholicism. Nativist opposition to Catholic immigration fluctuated after 1825, but it never disappeared.")

CHAPTER 12

THE PROCEDURAL CONTEXT OF CONSTITUTIONAL LITIGATION

■ ■ ■

12–4 NONTAXPAYER STANDING

12–4.3 CONGRESSIONAL STANDING

Unabridged, p. 1507; add to end of *Notes*, new Note 4:

4. *Arizona State Legislature v. Arizona Independent Redistricting Commission*, 576 U.S. ___, 135 S.Ct. 2652, 192 L.Ed.2d 704 (2015). In 2000, the voters of Arizona approved a ballot initiative to remove all redistricting authority from the state legislature and transfer it to an independent redistricting commission. They sought to prevent partisan gerrymandering of congressional legislative districts. The State legislature sued claiming that the initiative for congressional districting violates the Elections Clause (U.S. Const., Art. I, § 4, cl. 1), which provides that the times, places and manner of congressional elections "shall be prescribed in each State by the *Legislature* thereof" unless Congress alters such laws or regulations. The Arizona legislature argued that it "must have at least the opportunity to engage (or decline to engage) in redistricting before the State may involve other actors in the redistricting process." (The Arizona redistricting commission also drew state legislative districts, but that raises no issue under the Elections Clause.)

Ginsburg, J., for the Court (5 to 4), held, first, the legislature had standing to sue because its claim that the voter proposition stripped it of constitutional authority was a concrete and particularized injury. *Raines v. Byrd* (1997) held that "*six individual Members* of Congress lacked standing to challenge the Line Item Veto Act." In contrast, the Arizona Legislature "is an institutional plaintiff asserting an institutional injury, and it commenced this action after authorizing votes in both of its chambers."

On the merits, the Court held that the Elections Clause does not preclude a voter initiative that creates an alternative way of redistricting. "The dominant purpose" of the Elections Clause "was to empower Congress to override state election rules, not to restrict the way States enact legislation." The Court rejected the argument that the word "legislature" means the representative body that makes the laws of the people. "The exercise of the initiative, we acknowledge, was not at issue in our prior decisions." Nonetheless, "we see no constitutional barrier to a State's empowerment of its people by embracing that form of lawmaking." The Court should not interpret the Elections Clause "to single out federal elections as the one area in which States may not use citizen initiatives as an alternative legislative process."

The Court emphasized the public policy in favor of taking redistricting away from the legislature. While the redistricting commissions have not eliminated partisan suspicions associated with political line-drawing, they limit the conflict of interest when the legislature controls redistricting. They "impede legislators from choosing their voters instead of facilitating the voters' choice of their representatives."

Roberts, C.J., dissented, joined by Scalia, Thomas and Alito, JJ., arguing that the Court decision has "no basis in the text, structure, or history of the Constitution," which "contains seventeen provisions referring to the 'Legislature' of a 'State,' many of which cannot possibly be read to mean 'the people.' " The 17th Amendment "transferred power to choose United States Senators from "the Legislature" of each State, Art. I, § 3, to 'the people thereof.' The Amendment resulted from an arduous, decades-long campaign in which reformers across the country worked hard to garner approval from Congress and three-quarters of the States. What chumps! Didn't they realize that all they had to do was interpret the constitutional term 'the Legislature' to mean 'the people'?"

Scalia and Thomas each filed separate dissents, and joined each other's dissents, arguing the legislature lacks standing to assert a claim against another entity of state government. Scalia added that he would normally not express an opinion on the merits, but the majority's resolution is "so utterly devoid of textual or historic support" that he "cannot avoid adding my vote to the devastating dissent of the Chief Justice."